HOW TO ORGANIZE
A CHILDREN'S LIBRARY

by
DOROTHY H. CURRIE
Supervisor of School Libraries and
Audio-Visual Instructional Materials.
Yonkers Public Schools
Yonkers, New York

Oceana Publications, Inc.
Dobbs Ferry, New York
1965

For

Aunt Tena, who taught me that there are many ways to do what does not seem possible, and for

Stephen, who taught me that to do what is possible is an exciting privilege.

CONTENTS

CONTENTS

PREFACE

This book is not for the technical professional. It is for the professional educator who is not a trained librarian; it is for the interested amateur. It is for the many parents who have worked in school libraries because they have believed it was important to do so. It is for the teacher who has felt that taking time to help arrange library materials or to help buy new books or to bring her students to the library is important. It is for the men and women, the boys and girls who have been interested in starting and nurturing libraries in clubs, in churches, in hospitals, in their own homes, or wherever there was need for a library. It is for anyone who doesn't know how and who wants to learn.

It is also for someone who doesn't have very much help to begin with. This book is the help you may need. That is its intention.

If it can solve your problem, it has been worth doing. If it doesn't give you the answer but helps you work out the answer for yourself, excellent. If it seems to be contrary to something you have learned about somewhere else, that, too, is good, for there are many ways of doing a job and there are many different solutions to problems. One of the qualities of a good librarian is the ability to recognize what needs to be done and to see the simplest way to do it.

The significant and lasting test when you have to make a choice is: "Does this let the job which I am supposed to do get done?" Read, ask the questions, and then make the decision that is right for you and for your library.

Acknowledgment is made to the following: Dr. Stanley S. Wynstra, Superintendent of Schools, Yonkers, N.Y., for his encouragement and assistance in developing the parent volunteer program in our school system; the many parents for their participation in the program and for their responses to it; Arnold Winegarden for his generosity in giving his time and skills to the photography; the H. W. Wilson Company for permission to reproduce samples of its printed catalog cards and to use examples from its other publications; the Forest Press, Inc., for permission to reproduce parts of the Dewey Decimal Classification and Relative Index; the Bro-Dart Industries for their generous copyright release to use samples of their products and their sketches showing the use of plastic book covers; the Library Bureau of Remington Rand to use illustrations of their processing supplies; the American Library Association to reproduce a sample entry from their *Basic Book Collection for Elementary Grades;* Demco Library Supplies, Gaylord Brothers, and Fordham Equipment Company for permission to use samples of their library supplies to demonstrate the various phases of book processing; the staff of Oceana Press for their courtesy and practical help in the preparation of the manuscript.

1

Getting Started

Recognizing the Need

Twelve years ago the author was faced with the kind of problem which this book tries to do something about—elementary schools without librarians, various kinds of book collections in various kinds of order and disorder, or even no books at all.

This problem is not limited to our community. In September of 1964 a report issued by the United States Office of Education pointed out that in this country during the school year 1962-1963 a little more than seventy-four percent of all schools had centralized libraries. Or, to put this in reverse, one fourth of all schools do not have centralized libraries. The report also indicated that elementary schools do not fare as well as secondary school—only 57.8 percent, which is a little more than half, of the elementary schools have centralized libraries. These figures all refer to public schools and public school systems.

There is need, too, according to this report, for librarians. It states that, "while 93 percent of secondary schools with libraries are served by school librarians, only 51 percent of elementary schools with centralized libraries were so served."

If we take this one step farther, we learn that there are

almost 60,000 elementary schools, public elementary schools, in this country. Using the above figures, we may arrive at the fact that 25,320 schools do not have centralized libraries and 42,314 schools do not have librarians. Or we can say that of the 34,680 elementary schools which do have libraries, only 17,686 have librarians.

However we may report the figures, the situation is one which is not good for the educational opportunities of boys and girls in those schools which do not have libraries or which do not have librarians. The quality of education of these young people is not good enough for today's world. For the world of tomorrow it is dangerously close to poor.

One Approach to a Problem

How, then, can someone—anyone—who cares about the need for libraries for young people begin to do something to improve the situation? Probably the most wished-for solution would be to see, in the decision-makers, a willingness to provide money for staff, money for materials, money for space, money for supplies, and leadership in establishing and developing library program.

Barring that happy solution, the next approach is to try to persuade the decision-makers that providing for a part of the need will let the beginnings of program develop. This will require the establishing of priorities in terms of the values which will come from whatever is selected. The priority value should be related to what will do most to improve the quality of the educational program. This will be as varied as the situations which exist, and some examination of these situations will be needed to arrive at an intelligent choice.

For us, the greatest need was money for books. Supplies, space, staff—these were secondary and their scarcity or non-existence was, to say the least, awkward. But without books no aspects of program at all would have been possible. Principals and the various local Parent-Teacher Associations supplied the money for the book pockets, date due slips, book cards, paste, ink, etc.

Then came the critical period—could we succeed in getting help from our community? We asked for help and we listed the kinds of skills which were needed and which we could not take time to teach—typing, for example. Aside from the special skills of the few, there were two basic requirements which we asked everyone to meet—a willingness to work regularly over an extended period of time, and a willingness to learn the various processes and steps involved in the organization of libraries. These two characteristics are fundamental in recruiting volunteers and should help in selecting the individuals who will form the core of the group. Without them, the volunteer program will, in itself, create problems and additional supervisory time will be needed.

Those who wish to work at shorter intervals, less regularly perhaps, can also make a contribution, but the basic movement of the program will rely on consistent work over a longer time period.

This suggests that it is important to have some means of training others directly or indirectly. The knowledge, the know-how which makes the program possible, must be available. Professional guidance, either in the person of a certificated librarian or one who has worked in libraries, or in the form of printed or visual learning materials, is necessary. For it is urgent that the skills and the knowledge embodied in the librarian or the book be extended to the volunteers so that they may become skilled. The true test of the teaching and learning is, in this program, as it is in all educational programs—can the learner continue to function in the learning area without direct supervision?

If the services of professional librarians or trained individuals are available, workshops may be conducted for large or small groups. These workshops may be held at suitable intervals to train volunteers in the sequences of processing

books and establishing necessary records. They may be used
to reinforce the skills after the learning has occurred. It
may be necessary or desirable, also, to give encouragement
and support and appreciation when the pressures of problems become too wearisome to face alone.

It should not be assumed that when the non-professional
carries out these basic library operations he usurps the functions of the professionally trained librarian. Indeed, the
experience in establishing the volunteer assistants' program
and in conducting the training program for the assistants
has served to crystallize from the masses of work any librarian faces those tasks and those operations which demand
extensive professional education and specialized knowledge.
It has helped define those skills which can, by their very
nature, accrue only to the professional librarian. This pin-
pointing of the professional functions of the librarian is
readily understood and accepted by the non-professional
worker. The clear distinction of what can be learned without exposure to a long and arduous educational sequence
enhances, in fact, the unique contributions of the professional librarian. The result is a deeper appreciation of the
work of the librarian. There is no longer a feeling that the
librarian is a care-taker of books or a staff person who has
"nothing to do because he has no classes." The librarian,
instead, is now recognized as a professional educator whose
skills and function reach into every grade level and into
every subject area, providing educational opportunity and
educational guidance for student and teacher alike.

At the same time, those tasks so necessary for the smooth
operation of a library, which can be learned by the non-
professional, are accomplished with considerably less pain
because of the consistent interest and concern and hard
work of the lay assistant. As a result, the professional librarian who is fortunate enough to have this help is permitted
to use his time for those purposes which cannot otherwise
be fulfilled.

This book takes the place of the workshops and the training programs which have been used. It is written on a broader scale than would be necessary for our own school system. It is, at the same time, more specific about particular sequences and more general about the various approaches to these sequences. This is necessary in order to be able to indicate the many different ways of doing a job and to allow the user to select the best possible way to adapt the information and apply it to his own particular case.

The user is advised to skip over the parts of this guide which he does not need, and to concentrate on those parts which pertain to his own situation or which prove to give him the needed instruction and the precise guidance for making decisions. It is advisable for the user to begin to build in his own situation an orderly pattern of work sequences and to establish overall procedures which help set up a functional library for whatever purposes exist in each different case. Read, experiment, reject or accept, try again, and succeed. Your goal should be your balancing point in making any choices.

The Basic Guides

From time to time it will be necessary to refer to the authorities and the authoritative materials accepted as basic in school libraries. The following list contains the titles referred to in the text. These books are practically indispensable and must be available. This will be true whether or not a professionally trained librarian is involved in the program.

BASIC REFERENCE MATERIALS FOR PROCESSING LIBRARY BOOKS

Akers, Susan G. *Simple Library Cataloging*. American Library Association, 1954. Fourth edition. $5.00. (50 E. Huron St., Chicago, Ill.) Explains and illustrates the process of cataloging for the nonprofessional assistant in the school library.

American Library Association. *A.L.A. Rules for Filing Catalog Cards.*
A.L.A., 1942. $2.00.
Establishes rules for filing according to the most generally
accepted usage in American libraries.

American Library Association. *A Basic Book Collection for Elementary
Grades.* A.L.A., 1960. Seventh edition. $2.00.
Useful as a guide in buying books for a well-balanced collection
of books for an elementary school. Also valuable in helping the
non-professional in cataloging and classification.

Children's Catalog. H. W. Wilson, 1961. price varies, depending upon
enrollment of school. For non-existent schools or for administrative use allow about $8.00. (950 University Ave., N.Y. 52)
A comprehensive list of some 3300 books, both fiction and non-
fiction. Useful as a buying guide, for cataloging, for classification.
Kept up-to-date by yearly supplements. Main volume re-issued
(revised) every five years. If only one book can be purchased, this
is the first choice.

Dewey, Melvil. *Dewey Decimal Classification and Relative Index.*
Forest Press, 1959. Eighth abridged edition. $8.00. (Lake Placid
Club, Lake Placid, N.Y.)
Basic reference for classification, using the system most widely
used in public schools' libraries in the United States. Used in
many school libraries in other countries.

Gardiner, Jewel. *Administering Library Service in the Elementary
School.* A.L.A., 1954. Second edition. $3.50.
Helpful suggestions for organizing a library in the elementary
school.

Rue, Eloise, and La Plante, Effie. *Subject Headings for Children's
Materials.* A.L.A., 1952. $4.00.
Valuable both in classification and cataloging materials for chil-
dren's libraries.

The books on this list may be ordered directly from the publishers
at these addresses:

American Library Association
50 East Huron Street, Chicago 11, Illinois

H. W. Wilson Company
950 University Avenue, New York, N.Y., 10052

Forest Press, Inc.   (Publications of this company are also
    Lake Placid Club   from the H.W. Wilson Company, listed
    Lake Placid, N.Y.   above.)

Clearing the Way

If the library you are concerned with is a part of an institution, it is more important that you contact the individual or the group of people who are responsible for its operation. Be prepared to approach them with a concise statement of what you would like to do, how you think you can go about doing it, why you are interested in making this contribution, and what your purpose is. It should be stressed that any such statement needs to embody the relation of the library to the purposes of the institution. You will need permission to do what you want to do. You will also need the support of those who are the administrators and the decision-makers for this institution.

Be definite about what you think such a program will require in the way of understanding, financial support, and facilities. It is absolutely necessary, for your work and for your legal status, to have approval of what you want to do before you start to do it. This is particularly true if you will become involved in spending moneys or in working with others in the name of the organization. The size of the organization does not matter—it may be large or small. But the way must be opened, and the directions understood, both by you and the leaders of the group if you are to be successful in your undertaking.

For a school system, approach the Superintendent of schools. He is probably the authority empowered to grant permission to work in the schools and to do this particular job. If, at his discretion, permission also needs to be given by a principal or other staff officer, he will probably refer you to such persons. At any rate, this is the first step to take.

When the proper interest is shown by the authorizing persons and when encouragement is given, it then becomes the appropriate time to ask for the special kinds of cooperation necessary to provide money, facilities, and equipment. Only in this way will you be able to approach your work surely. It may be that decisions cannot be made on-the-spot.

Time may be needed to consider thoroughly all that may
be involved in such an undertaking. Decisions cannot be
pushed. Normally, the educator who is convinced that help
is offered only in the interests of improving educational
opportunities beyond what can be provided by the institution, itself, are willing to grant permission. Such permission
may be tentative, limited, or controlled. But communication
must continue and the doors of mutual effort and concern
must be opened and remain open.

Try to discover, also, whether or not limits are to be
placed on your contributions. It may be that you, the giver,
will establish limits; or it may be that these will be established by others. Certainly, limits are desirable. Whatever
these are, be aware of how they influence your approach to
the job. It may be that only a part of a goal may be
approached. Or it may be that a series of steps can be
developed which will let the work move progressively
through its various stages.

Discover, also, to whom you will be responsible. Rarely,
in any school system or in any school situation is anything
done by anyone without a formal or informal reporting of
work done, problems met and solved, problems still existing. Unless you have an absolutely free hand, it is important for the work that others understand the progress and
that they are involved with the progress. This will serve to
give support to you and to your work. It will also serve to
establish good rapport with these others, enabling you to
explain the real meaning of library services and the work
necessary to make these services available.

The library, finally established, will probably gain from
this mutual understanding. Whenever we wish to do something for someone else, it must be presented in terms of
their needs, their interests, their obligations. Otherwise,
service has no meaning. The services must be for others in
their terms, and must be given in that manner.

You are now ready to set up a definite schedule. Establishing regular hours and regular days not only points to your own sincerity in giving huge amounts of time, but also it points to a business-like approach toward the work. This regularity and this obvious understanding of the extent of the work will help build confidence in others toward the program.

Know, also, where you will be doing the work. Organize your space for work and treat whatever space you have as an office area, leaving it neat and orderly after each work session.

Do not be discouraged at any delays or at any seeming reluctance to let you begin immediately. School systems are not used to having laymen volunteer to conduct and carry out long-time programs. The idea that self-trained laymen, or even that laymen under professional supervision can actually perform useful services is not an idea that all educators accept readily. And there are, too, librarians, good and efficient and effective librarians, who may be skeptical of the value of such assistance. There are, too, people in administrative positions who cannot imagine teaching someone else to do the work they are doing, even if by so doing they become freer to do other more important work. It is difficult for some people to delegate work to anyone else. Such people will need to be convinced that what they have learned can be learned by someone else, even if that learning changes a bit in structure, in scope, in approach, in manner.

Certainly there is an area for reasonable doubt when we consider the technical rather than the mechanical processes of library work. Perhaps the reassurance lies in recognizing the limitations of the non-professional in the technical areas and in admitting that these limitations are reached fairly soon. These processes—classification and cataloging—will need to remain at a fairly simple level, and extensive use will have to be made of prepared or easily adaptive professionally prepared materials. Anything less than perfection may not be desirable, but it may be practical.

Such pre-conceived opinions and planning sequences may undergo a complete readjustment as the program moves, tentatively, into its first stages. Keeping an open and critical mind, however, can help evaluate the approaches to each phase of the sequences of work as they are developed, and new ideas can help rearrange the old ones to create a more acceptable program. Develop plans, yes. Change plans, yes. Know what is good about any situation and how to improve it. Keep your eye on your goals. Remember that you are doing a business-like project and that you need to remain business-like about it.

Ready to start? You have already started. You have thought about a problem and have been aware that it can be improved. You have stirrings of interest in improving it— deep stirrings if you have reached this far. From here, there is work, but work so satisfying that it is welcome.

Summary of Steps to Take

1. Get approval from the proper authority.
   a. Know what needs to be done.
   b. Know what you will need to do it—supplies, materials, information.
   c. Know how to go about doing it and have a manual or guide or person to help you learn how to do the job.

2. Get clearance for space to work.

3. Find out what you will have to work with: typewriter, supplies, or money for supplies, catalog cabinet, people.

4. Check to see if basic references are available or if money is available for their purchase.

5. Establish a regular work schedule. This may involve many or few hours each week, but make it regular—certain hours on certain days.

6. Know the kind of group who will use the library and how it fits into their needs.

7. Start the work, following the sequence in this manual or establishing some other sequence under other direction.

2

Assembling the Book Collection

Purposes of Book Selection

It is important and vital that all libraries for children be used to give more information about a subject than the child has available at home or in textbooks or from others sources. It is also important to have books which provide interesting reading about the topics which are the personal interest of the child. These kinds of books help keep the student reading for pleasure as well as for information. The development of this kind of reading habit—for fun—is one of the goals of the educational program.

Every library needs to provide authoritative material which can be used to find correct answers to specific questions. In a school library these materials should cover many subject areas. In other libraries the depth and breadth of the areas covered will depend upon the purposes of the library. Regardless of the type of library, however, the desired information should be available easily and quickly.

Every library needs to provide authoritative material which lets a boy or girl read more about a subject in depth and in breadth—going into this subject in detail and includ-

11

ing more facets of it. In other words, the books in the library should help a child stretch his mind.

The library is, indeed, the cultural center of a school. Here there should be available the records of the best of man's creations and thoughts from all historical periods. There should be man's contributions and developments in music, in art, in literature, in ideas he has held about himself, in his concepts of the universe, in his beliefs about religion and the morality of man.

To fulfill all these obligations requires that we select the collection. If we do not know how to select books for all these purposes and if we do not know very much about children's books, we will need to know how to use the prepared materials to assist us.

Because book collections are assembled in different ways, we need to know, too, how to select from each list or each collection and how to select for all the potential interests of all the students. If this particular task can be accomplished, there will be an acceptable and good collection when we finish.

Weeding the Collections

We use this expression—weeding the collection—to describe the process of examining what we have and discarding what we do not want. Obviously, it must apply to a collection which already exists. An inherited collection may be in one place, physically, or it may be spread through many different locations. It may be in one room—a storeroom, a classroom, a closet, or wherever there is space; it may be in boxes, packed away and waiting for attention; it may be in a hallway; it may be that the collection is not yet together, but is waiting for someone to take over the responsibility to put these scattered materials together to become a library. It may be that people who have these small scattered bits of materials will be happy or unhappy at what they may consider giving up "their" possessions, even though the giving up is temporary and even though it results in having more materials available when the work is completed. Persuasion or the fiat can bring the books together; experience will let the mind and the emotions eventually recognize the good which lies in this new pattern.

Gift collections are another, kind of inherited collection, and like them may be housed anywhere. They may also consist of several separate collections, all waiting to be assembled and organized as one group. They may be just a promise, and not yet actually available.

None of these groups of materials is, actually, a library collection as yet. Rather, these are groups of books from which the titles to be added to the library will be chosen. This choosing is selection; the process of eliminating the undesirable books is the weeding.

Selection is usually made, first, with the purpose of the library in mind. It is possible for a group which has one area of activity as its special interest to establish a library whose materials are so selected that they fit into the limited purposes of the group. Recreational bodies, for example, might assemble a collection of books which are all about hobbies and other recreational activities. Or a literary club might select one general type of literary form such as poetry or novels or literary criticsm. A musical club might develop a library of books only about music—composers' lives, books about performing artists, books about musical forms or about special musical editions, about musical instruments, or about music appreciation. Specialized organizations will be very careful to add to their libraries only those titles which fit into the general purposes of the group.

Groups wishing a general collection covering many different kinds of reading interests will select from gifts and donations in another way. The general suitability of the book will be a very important consideration. Books which are too childish, too scholarly, too highly technical, too "off-beat" may be out of place in a collection of this sort.

One of the problems which may arise when materials are offered as gifts to a library collection pertains to the disposition of the materials—will everything offered be found in the collection? It should be established early in the life of a library and rigidly adhered to through its existence that act of giving to the library does not mean total acceptance of the gift with automatic addition to the book collection. The final decision as to whether or not any particular title will become a part of the collection will depend upon the decision of the person or group responsible for assembling the collection and for its organization and for its operation. The rejection of a title may suggest that the book be returned or that it be disposed of otherwise. Generally, it will be well to indicate that the final selection will lie with the library personnel and that the disposition of the unacceptable materials will also lie with the library personnel. To take care of this early in the library's growth will avoid problems later.

There are, however, some very practical suggestions which can be helpful in making decisions about whether or not particular books should be added to the collection. These may be summarized as being the physical condition of the book, the format of the book, and the subject and treatment of the subject in the book. When any of the books do not meet the standards given here, the books should not be added to the collection.

1. The physical condition of the book:

   a. The book should be hard bound. Soft-covered books and paper-backs may be accepted for temporary addition to the collection, but should not be considered permanent additions. If paper-backs must be added as permanent acquisitions, they should be rebound or reinforced and provided with durable covers.

   b. The book should be firm in its covers. The contents should not sag away from the board covers, and there should be no loose sections of paging which tend to drop away from the rest of the contents.

    c. The outside cover should be clean and without scratches or cuts. Light soil may be removed, but dirt which has been ground into the cloth or the paper of the cover cannot be removed.

    d. Notice especially the top and the bottom of the "spine" of the book. This is the part of the book which holds the front and back covers together, and into which the contents of the book are fitted. If these edges are torn or frayed, do not accept the book unless it is a highly valuable and rare item.

    e. There should be few, if any, loose pages.

    f. The pages of the book should be clean and without tears.

    g. The pages should not be "dog-eared"—that is, bent over at the top and bottom outside edges or corners of the page.

2. How the book is made:

    a. The size of the print should be suitable for the people who will use the library. Small children read larger print more easily than small print. Older children will prefer smaller type, and few children will choose to read books with very small type.

    b. The pictures should be good illustrations or photographs. They should not be distorted unless the book is a highly imaginative one and is using this technique for a specific purpose, such as to depict imaginative creatures. Such distortion may also be keyed to the subject of the book, and, in that case, it is acceptable.

    c. The colors of the pictures should help carry out the ideas of the book and should not be "muddied."

    d. The paper should be of good quality. One way to check this is to see if the paper has a spongy texture. If it does, it is soft and will aborb soil readily and will, usually, begin to yellow and become brittle.

    e. The cover material, also, should be of good quality so that it will bear handling by children for about five years. This is the normal life of the book which is used and handled normally.

3. What the book is about:

    a. The subject of the book should be suitable for the collection.

    b. The book should not be "out-of-date" in terms of its subject. For instance, some science books and some books about the nations of the world need to be fairly new if they are to be considered accurate. Whenever a book's subject undergoes rapid change or development or expansion, the books on that subpect will need to be fairly new.

    c. The book should be written on a level suitable for the people
who will use it. The vocabulary of a young child may not
be as extensive as that of an older child. Further, the way
in which sentences are put together and the ways in which
ideas are developed should be suitable tor fhe children who
will be using the materials.

    d. The writing in the book should be correct in grammar and
in sentence structure. An exception to this lies in the area of
fiction, and in books of fiction the conversation of the
characters may be quite ungrammatical and quite incorrect.

    e. The style of writing should lead the reader easily from one
idea to another in an interesting manner. There are many
different styles of writing. Each author has his own, and may
even have several different styles for different kinds of content. There is no easy way to test the quality of style except
by reading it and by "feeling" it and by examining it.

If all of the above standards are met, we can move along
to the next test. This may be applied to books for school
libraries. It may be used also for other children's collections,
but its major use will be for school library collections first,
and for public library collections for children second.

Basic Lists for School Libraries

There are several good lists of books which include recommended titles for children's library collections. These lists
have been developed by groups of professional librarians,
teachers, and other educators. They are kept up-to-date by
a process of constant revision, based upon continuous examination of new books and, after evaluating them, by
regular publication of new and revised lists at specific intervals. These lists are very helpful in many ways. They may be
used to help select books or weed out books from a miscel-
laneous collection. They have other uses, too, and these will
be mentioned as we have need to use the lists for these
purposes.

All the titles which are included in these lists are important for school libraries to have—especially school libraries
of the United States—and these lists should be used in buying and maintaining the basic collections. Even professional

librarians make extensive use of them and rely upon the assistance they provide.

These lists may also be of value in any English-speaking community, although they may not, for other countries, list the titles one should select for first purchase. Non-American countries which use the English language and non-English speaking countries frequently have their own basic lists. A check with the national governmental body responsible for the educational program in each country (or its regional or local office) will provide this information. If no basic lists are available, this governmental agency will probably be able to refer you to the basic lists which are used or to someone who can indicate what the basic lists are.

Because of their importance, each of the basic lists developed for school and public libraries for young people in the United States is described in detail. It is recommended that as you read the descriptions, you turn to the book and verify the statement's claim by examination of the book. Do this for each section of each book, also, as the description is given.

The lists which will be described in this section include:

Elementary School Library Lists: *Children's Catalog*
                                   A Basic Book Collection for
                                         Elementary Grades
                                   State and local lists
                                   Lists of Educational Groups

Junior High School Library Lists: *Children's Catalog*
                                    Standard Catalog for High School Libraries
                                    A Basic Book Collection for Junior High Schools
                                   State and local lists

Senior High School Library Lists: Lists issued by educational groups
                                    Standard Catalog for High School Libraries
                                    A Basic Book Collection for Senior High Schools
                                   State and local lists
                                   Lists issued by educational groups

The *Children's Catalog* and the *Standard Catalog*, both, are publications of the H. W. Wilson Company and both are similar in the kind of material presented and the way in which it is presented. They are lists of books, primarily of American publishers and in English, with each presenting titles suitable for the grade and age levels which are indicated in the listings above. Each publication is issued in a large volume at 5-year intervals, but the two do not have the same 5-year period covered. Each is kept up-to-date by yearly supplements issued in the intervals between the large revision periods.

Each of these books has 5 major parts which are alike, but which do not, necessarily, appear in the same sequence within the book. Each book, in addition, has some parts which are not found in the other. The *Children's Catalog*, for example, includes a graded list of books suitable for the reading levels K-9. Another section in this volume is the list of so-called "easy" books--books with simple vocabulary, large print, and a large proportion of pictures. These two sections are not found in the *Standard Catalog*. On the other hand, the *Standard Catalog* includes a list of magazines suitable for use in secondary school libraries. This list is not separate from the book listings in the *Children's Catalog*.

The major parts to be found in each of these books are as follows:

1. An introductory section on how to use the various parts of the book. This is helpful and will supplement the descriptions which are included here.

2. A list of the major divisions of the Dewey Decimal Classification System. More detail will be given in Chapter VII, which is concerned with how books are classified. Look over this list, see how each part is related to the other parts. This manual will discuss each of these parts and show how they fit together. Study the system now and then, later on, as the step-by-step explanation is made, it will make wonderful sense and will be most helpful to you as you work with the books.

3. An alphabetic listing of books—alphabetically by the author, by the titles, and by the subjects of the various books in the lists. Note that all of these are in one list. This alphabetic arrangement is an index to the "classified list" described next. You should take particular notice of the number in heavy type which follows the listing of any title. This is the Dewey Decimal Classification number for the book. It is included so that the user may refer to the classified lists of the books and find the complete description of the information for each title.

4. A list of books, arranged by numbers as in our numbering system. Each of these numbers has a meaning, and these meanings were suggested in the Dewey Decimal Classification System list mentioned in item 2 in this description. Note that Arabic numerals are used and that different numbers are assigned to the different subject areas. This section lists the books first by the assigned classification number, and within the same classification group, alphabetically by author. It includes the title as found on the title page of the book, information about the edition of the book, the illustrator, the publishing date, the publisher, the cost at the time of publication. It also indicates whether or not the book is part of a series or a set. Here, too, is found a summary of the contents and a description of the treatment of the subject, written, usually, by a professional librarian or professional reviewer. Next come the suggested subjects or catalog headings which describe the book's contents and any "added" entries. These added entries will be discussed in Chapter VIII.

5. A graded list of books appears in the *Children's Catalog*. It is not found in the *Standard Catalog*. This granting is done in such a way that several grade levels are included in each list, making it more helpful to librarians, teachers, and parents in relating suitable materials to children of different grade and reading levels.

6. A list of publishers and their addresses. This list lends itself to many uses. It will be most helpful, probably, in ordering books. The most recent listing of the publishers would be used since there have been mergers of several publishers during the past few years.

These publications of the H. W. Wilson Company are major references and should be purchased as soon as there is money of any kind available for any purchases. They will be referred to often, and the user of this manual should assume that what is said about one will apply to the other. We may refer to the *Children's Catalog*, the *Standard Cata-*

log or the "Wilson Catalog" interchangeably. It is a bit unwieldy to name both titles when we suggest that you use the one which applies to your library's users. Consequently, whenever we use any one of the above names, you should interpret it to mean the particular catalog of the Wilson Company which you are using.

A Basic Book Collection for Elementary Grades, A Basic Book Collection for Junior High Schools, and *A Basic Book Collection for Senior High Schools:* These titles are all publications of the American Library Association and list titles which are basic for school libraries of the various levels. These lists are revised from time to time and their information supplements that given in the Wilson catalogs. There is some duplication of titles, but there are also many different titles. Professional school librarians and professional librarians who are authorities in the area of books for young people of various ages and school libraries have worked together on selection committees, reviewing and evaluating the titles of many new books before developing the lists.

These books, like the Wilson series, are similar in format, in organization, and content. There are two major listings of books in each—the alphabetic listing and the classified listing. The information is similar to that included in the Wilson lists.

In the case of these publications, we will use the general term "A.L.A. list" or Basic "A.L.A. list" interchangeably with the full names of the listings. And we will expect the user to refer, in such cases, to the list published by the American Library Association which is suitable for the particular grade and age level of the students and young people who are the users of the library.

State and Local Lists: It will be important to discover whether or not the State Department of Education of your state or the Board of Education of your community has issued a basic list for school library collections. Some cities have their own approved lists of titles for school libraries. Others do not. Some schools or other institutions may be under the control of other types of governing bodies so that approval of titles will depend upon the approval by the proper authorities of such agencies. If your particular library is for a private school or for an institution, check to see if you need to use some approved list not mentioned here.

Lists of Educational Groups: Several specialized lists such as those issued by the American Association for the Advancement of Science or by the Association for Supervision and Curriculum Development are useful. They are not, however, substitutes for the Wilson and A.L.A. lists, but should be used to supplement these basic lists.

Governmental Agencies: Approved lists may also be issued by other governmental groups of other nations. Volunteer librarians who will be working in countries other than the United States will do well to consult with the proper authorities. It may be that there are special procedures for clearing titles for approval for either purchase or for acceptance as gifts. These suggestions should apply for libraries other than public school libraries, too.

Using the Basic Lists

A. *For Existing Collections:* After every title has passed the first screening process—for physical condition, for format, for content, for recency—it should be checked against the basic lists which apply—the Wilson list which is appropriate, the correct A.L.A. list, and any other necessary lists.

It will be helpful to follow this sequence:

1. Begin by checking the alphabetic listing to see if the title is included.

2. If the title is included, notice the classification number given after it in bold face type.

3. Using that classification number, turn to the classified section of the listing and, in the numbered sequence, look for the proper classification number for this book.

4. Check, then, by author and title to find the correct entry for the particular book you are working with.

5. If the title is listed, place a check (√) in front of the entry for the book in this classified section.

6. Check for each title in each listing.

7. Separate titles which are not included in any list from those which are included once or more. Someone will need to examine these unlisted books to see whether or not they are suitable for the library. It may be that you have been authorized to do this or it may be that someone on the professional staff of the school or institution will have to be responsible for this. If there should be any doubt, however, as to whether or not a particular title should be added to the collection, don't add it. Find a place to store the questionable titles, holding them until there is time for a more complete checking. The authorities must have delegated the responsible authority to you for making such decisions before you assume it.

8. Make out a work card for every book checked in the list and for every book which is to be added to the library. For a set of books with one title (such as a set of encyclopedia), make out one card. For a book which is part of a series, but which has a title of its own, different from the series title, make a separate card. See the form below and follow it in making out these cards. This is exactly like the form which will be used for ordering books, and such order cards become the work cards when the books are received.

Class No.	Author (surname first)
Accession No.	Finkel, Lawrence S. & Krawitz, Ruth
	Title How to study
No. of copies ordered	Volumes
Date ordered	Publisher and Place Oceana Publications - Dobbs Ferry, N.Y. Year 1964
Dealer	Edition or series No. of copies desired List Price 2 50 Cost
Date received	Department for which recommended
Date of bill	Teacher making request
L. C. card No.	Reviewed in
GAYLORD 101-S	PRINTED IN U.S.A.

ORDER CARD with basic information

9. Place the work card inside the front cover of the book. This card will go along with the book until it has been completely processed for addition to the library.

B. *For Buying New Collections:* This is the ideal situation which many librarians would like to be able to do, but which, actually, few have the opportunity to become involved with. Before beginning to make out order cards, based on selections of titles from the basic lists, it will be necessary to give consideration to the budget. This will be important in determining what is purchased first.

If, for example, you were to buy every book in the basic lists mentioned earlier, you would find some duplication and some differences in quoted prices. The following table gives you some idea of what funds are involved and the number of titles included. These figures reflect our editing.

Basic List	No. of Titles	Funds Needed
Children's Catalog, 1961 edition	3310	$12,000 Estim.
Children's Catalog, 1962 Supplement	360	1164.35
1963 Supplement	255	924.09
1964 Supplement	272	1040.64
A.L.A. Basic Book Collection, Elem.	1451	3785.91

This begins to give you some idea of the cost of a library collection. The amount of money given above is fairly accurate even though there may be some doubts as to the actual cost of the collection.

Normally, a school may purchase books for libraries at about two thirds of the market price. However, prices are subject to change overnight, so that prices listed in 1961 may be quite different at this time. Also, if a school buys from a jobber (and some school districts are required to put such orders out for competitive bidding) some titles will not be eligible for the discount price submitted by the jobber. Materials such as encyclopedias and several other types of materials must be purchased from the publisher's established representatives. These books will have special prices for schools which are not reflected in the over-all discount figures. Some of the titles listed in these basic collections will be out-of-print or out-of-stock and, therefore, not available from the jobber. These are a few of the kinds of problems which will be reflected in the financial planning for a new library.

And that is what comes first. If you will be purchasing a brand new library or a part of one, find out first of all how much money you will have available to pay for the books, the supplies, and any equipment.

Generally, if you cannot buy everything, it will be important to buy from the largest major list or from the mandated list. For public school libraries in the United States which are not operating in a system with its own approved list, the *Children's Catalog* is a good list to start from. If your situation is one requiring the use of an approved list, use it, following the general method of controlling the accounts.

It will be wise to allow one fourth to one fifth of the limited budget to basic references. If you can buy everything, you will not need to be concerned with this problem. If, on the other hand, you have a limited budget, use this method of selecting from the basic list:

1. Set aside about one fourth of the budget for the basic references and select them from the list at the end of this chapter, buying from the FIRST PURCHASE group before selecting from the other recommended titles.

2. Subtract this amount from the total allocation to get the working budget for the general collection.

3. Compute the percentage which this amount represents of the total amount in the basic list you will be using. If you are buying initially from the *Children's Catalog* list this will be the amount available from your budget over $15,000.

4. Reduce this fraction so that the numerator is 1 by dividing both the numerator and denominator by the numerator. Example: Suppose you have available the sum of $600. Use this over $15,000, to make a fraction: 600/15,000. Reduce this fraction (arithmetic) to 1/25.

5. This means that you will be able to buy every 25th book included in the basic list. Actually, you will want to substitute some titles for others in order to include books from every category, but the above is a good general guide.

If the book to be selected turns out to be a basic reference, take the next title on the list. If you find that you are skipping some categories completely, select a general book for that category and eliminate a book of fiction. It may be necessary to do this for several titles. This method will give you a balanced collection which the budget may have limited in number, but which will provide for a fractional representation of the total collection.

In preparing to order these books, the procedure to be followed should meet two tests: 1. It must conform to the business procedures of the school or institution in its requisitioning for purchases and in making payments. 2. It must provide a list of materials in a way which will permit the jobbers and the publishers to fill orders. There are many different ways, all suitable for particular systems. One method which works very well for those who will be doing buying from small budgets and which is simple to use involves the following steps:

1. As a title is selected from one of the basic lists, make an order card for it. See the sample "work card" illustrated in this chapter or use a form such as is shown. This card or one similar to it may be purchased from any library supply firm.

Class No.	Author (surname first)		
Accession No.	Title		
No. of copies ordered			Volumes
Date ordered	Publisher and Place		Year
Dealer	Edition or series No. of copies desired List Price Cost		
Date received	Department for which recommended		
Date of bill	Teacher making request		
L. C. card No.	Reviewed in		
GAYLORD 101-S	PRINTED IN U.S.A.		

The supply firms, listed on page 37, will, on request, send a catalog of their materials (which gives the costs for the various quantities) at your request and without charge.

2. As the card is made out for the book, pencil in a light check (√) in front of the title in the classified listing which you are using to prepare your orders. This black pencilled code will mean that the book is on order. When the book is received, the check is re-written either in ink or in colored pencil to indicate that the library has the title.

3. The order card, one for each title, needs to have the following information on it for the ordering process: author, title, publisher, date of publication, price, and the number of copies or the number of volumes (in a set). Books may be ordered without knowledge of the publication date and with incorrect prices, but the other information must be included.

4. In addition to these items, certain others must be added in order to make the order card fulfill the needs of the "work card" which it will become when the book is received. It will save time to include these things now rather than to have to go back later and fill them in. Include, therefore, the classification number from the basic list, any suggested subject headings, and some code to indicate that printed catalog cards are available. It will also be helpful to have the number of pages in the book and a note that the book has illustrations. The classification number is easily identified, since that is how the books are listed. The suggested subject headings will be found in small print below the description of the book. The availability of printing cards is indicated by a large W in the entry. It will be well to use a code on the order card to indicate this fact, and one simple way to do that is to write a red W in the upper right-hand corner of the card. Other items are provided for on the order cards.

    If it is necessary to use the back of the card to list the suggested subject headings given for the book, write the word "over" on the face of the order card, at the bottom.

5. When the order card is completed, put it into a file along with all the other order cards. Arrange these cards in the following manner:

    a. Alphabetically by publisher.
    b. Within one publisher's list, alphabetically by author.
    c. Within one publisher's list and one author's list, alphabetically by title.

This will bring all the books of one publisher together for transferring to the requisition forms and will simplify that part of the work.

6. If you do not have a card catalog cabinet or the proper kind of

filing drawer, use a shoe box to hold the cards and make index guides from pieces of cardboard. If you have some money available, it is possible to buy a heavy cardboard box file from a stationery store. This will give you the proper size and will be a neater looking file.

The next step will be to check with the administrative office of your institution or school to discover whether or not some regular requisition form is used. Regardless of what kind of form is used, it will be necessary to have the information given in this chapter for each book to identify your choice.

Because book ordering is different from any other kind of purchasing and because it involves so many individual items, special requisition forms for buying library books are used. The example given on the next page shows a satisfactory form. It is used in two different sizes—a short form about 8-1/2 inches x 6-1/2 inches and a long form about 8-1/2 inches by 13 inches. The short form is used when ordering less than ten titles; the long form for more than ten. A separate requisition is made for each firm with whom an order will be placed. For the jobber, the pages are typed in sequence, with several publishers included in the sequence.

Note that the information called for on this form is included on the order cards. At the time the requisitions are to be typed, check with the business department to learn how many copies of such lists they will need for their various records. Type this number of copies PLUS ONE. If the business offices need two copies, type three; if they need four copies, type five. This extra copy is for the library's records. The number of copies will vary from school district to school district and from institution to institution.

Here are samples of requisitions actually used in the ordering of books. Examine them and note the general instructions given at the top. Note also that one form has many different publishers listed. This is called the *jobber's order*. The other form has only one publisher's titles and it is called an *order direct*.

REPLACEMENTS		BOARD OF EDUCATION	REQ. NO.

REPLACEMENTS_____
NEW BOOKS___X___

BOARD OF EDUCATION
YONKERS, NEW YORK

REQ. NO._____
ACCOUNT General S.O.
            Libraries

REQUISITION FOR LIBRARY BOOKS

APPROVED: SCHOOL___# 30_____ DATE April 8 19 65

_____
DEPT. HEAD

_____   Trade Bindings Only   PRINCIPAL
BUS. ADMINISTRATOR

One copy each of the following titles:

No. of Copies	Author	Title	Publisher	Publication Date	List Price
	Hodges, C	Shakespeare's theatre	Coward	1964	5.00
	Fisher, A	In the middle of the night	Crowell	1965	3.75
	Fisher, A	Listen, rabbit	"	1964	3.50
	Hopkinson, F	Battle of the kegs	"	1964	3.75
	McCain, M	Writing	Farrar	1964	2.50
	Chaucer, G	A taste of Chaucer	Harcourt	1964	3.75
	Pack, R	How to catch a crocodile	Knopf	1964	3.25
	Ciardi, J	John J. Plenty & Fiddler Dan	Lippincott	1963	2.95
	Ciardi, J	You know who	"	1964	3.50
	Nash, O	Untold adventures of Santa Claus	Little	1964	2.95
	Faber, D	Robert Frost:America's poet	Prentice	1964	3.25
	Aldis, D	Is anybody hungry?	Putnam	1964	2.75
	Garten, J	Alphabet tale	Random	1964	2.50
	Larrick, N	Piper, pipe that song again	"	1965	1.95
	Cole, W	Birds & beasts were there	World	1963	4.95
					50.30

All The Above Books Received In Good Condition

_____   Date_____19____
SIGNATURE OF PRINCIPAL

| REPLACEMENTS_____ | **BOARD OF EDUCATION** | REQ. NO. **86-621** |
| NEW BOOKS__ X ____ | YONKERS. NEW YORK | ACCOUNT **Special Ordinance** |

REQUISITION FOR LIBRARY BOOKS

APPROVED: SCHOOL **Emerson JHS**   DATE **March 20, 64**

_____ DEPT. HEAD

_____ SUB. ADMINISTRATOR   **ORDER DIRECT** _____ PRINCIPAL

No. of Copies	Author	Title	Publisher	Publication Date	List Price
1	Craig, P	The captive sea	Chilton Bk. Co.	1964	6.50
1	Del Ray, L	The mysterious sky	E. Washington Square	1964	3.95
1	Latham, M	My animal kingdom	Philadelphia Pa.	1963	3.95
1	Quick, L	Book of agates and other quartz gems		1963	9.95
					24.35

All The Above Books Received In Good Condition

_____ SIGNATURE OF PRINCIPAL   Date_____ 19__

If you have no money and no printed requisition forms, the same information which is given on the sample forms may be typed on regular typing paper. You may wish to use this form as a model:

To: (Name of Jobber or Company)   (Address)
From: (Name of School or Institution)   (Address)
Request for: Library Book order of titles as listed below. One of each title unless otherwise specified. All books to be in publisher's bindings unless specified otherwise.
Prices: All prices given are List (Or NET for library bindings)
Deliver to: (Name of institution and address. Attention of: ————)
No deliveries to be made after: (give closing date for filling order)
Bill to: (Person or institution responsible for paying the bill)

| Author | Title | Publisher | Date | List |

If this form is used, it should be accompanied by a letter on the letterhead of the school or institution written by the head of the institution to verify the authenticity of the order.

Still another way of handling the ordering of books is to use order slips instead of order cards. These are available from any library supply house, and come with several forms to a sheet and with several sheets held together for multiple copies of the form. Carbon paper is inserted in the assembling or carbon ink is used so that several copies are made at one typing. One of these copies is sent to the jobber or the book company and the other several copies may be used for various other purposes—temporary shelf list cards, temporary catalog cards, accounting records, etc.

It is recommended that you use the simpler method of ordering books, using the order cards and requisition forms unless you have plenty of staff to handle the filing of these slips and the maintenance of all files. The typing of the several copies of long requisition forms may seem awkward, but it is actually quite simple and may be handled quite effectively by the non-professional volunteer.

Do not be afraid to develop other simpler methods if you can. Remember that in the methods described, not only are the orders handled, but the business aspects of orders and payment and accounting have also been considered.

3

Business Aspects of Book Buying

Placing Book Orders

If the Board of Education is going to pay for the materials to be ordered, it is probably a matter of law or school board policy that purchases must be made in a particular way. Some school districts require that various companies must submit prices to the board before orders may be placed so that the board may select the business firm giving the best price for the quality of the article requested or for the exact material or equipment ordered. When library orders are to be placed, it is important to know what needs to "go into bid" and what does not have to be ordered in this way.

Usually, for book orders the exact titles are not issued for bid. Rather, the amount of money involved in the total purchasing job is stated and the jobbers or book suppliers return in a statement on a legal form to the board of education indicating how much discount they will allow on the various books. These may include trade books, text books, reference books, special editions of books, and special bindings. There may be more special kinds of books, but these are some of the common ones. Usually only trade books—

books that you can buy in a book store, no special bindings, books published for the general public—are required to be subjected to the bid process.

Trade books may carry from one third up to forty-five per cent discount. These upper bracket discounts are rare, but occasionally they exist. On the other hand, most librarians can buy books at one third off merely by ordering them on school stationery. Special bindings, usually reinforced bindings, and special editions usually have prices with no discount. These are called NET prices and books with NET prices usually may be ordered either from the jobber or from the company issuing the book at the identical price. Textbooks are usually available only from the publisher and so are most of the special reference books. The customary discount for texts (except in quantity) is 10%. Most special reference books have net prices for libraries, depending upon the quantity, and these must be ordered from the publishers.

It is important to know the business background to library purchasing and to use this information in typing the requisition forms. As the typing proceeds, it is necessary to order the books which cannot be supplied from the jobber's stock directly from the publisher or his agent. These are the ORDER DIRECT requisitions as compared with the JOBBERS ORDER.

Some common types of materials which are ordered directly from the publisher or his agent are given below. This listing does not include every possible type, but it is a workable list.

1. Any sets of encyclopedias, their supplements, and their yearbooks.
   Examples:
   a. Standard encyclopedias for children's use:
      1. Britannica Junior
      2. Compton's Pictured Encyclopedia
      3. World Book Encyclopedia
   b. Special subject area encyclopedias
      Children's Science Encyclopedia (Children's Press)

2. Large unabridged dictionaries or 1-volume encyclopedias
   Examples:
   Webster's Unabridged Dictionary
   Funk and Wagnall's Unabridged Dictionary
   Lincoln Library of Essential Information

3. Statistical Yearbooks
   Examples:
   World Almanac
   Political Handbook of the World

4. Books in special library bindings.
   Most prebinds or library bound books sell at a net price. This price may be different from the trade edition price. Many companies have both editions—trade and library—and the desired edition should be specified. Furthermore, some companies specialize in buying the unbound books from publishers and then issue them in special library bindings.
   Examples:
   Follett Publishing Company. 1010 W. Washington Boulevard. Chicago 7, Illinois.
   Don R. Phillips. Vandalia, Michigan.
   New Method Bindery, Inc. W. Morton Road. Jacksonville, Illinois.
   E. M. Hale & Co. Eau Claire, Wisconsin.
   Story House Corporation. Charlottesville, New York.
   There are many other companies providing this service and it will be well to try to discover some firm in your locality.
   There are also books published by large companies in library bindings and these should be ordered direct from the publishers.
   Examples:
   Harper & Brothers. (Harpercrest edition).
   Franklin Watts, Inc.
   Henry Z. Walck, Inc.
   Children's Press.
   Melmot Publications.

5. College and university press publications are usually ordered direct.

6. Reference books, published by regular publishers, carrying net prices.
   Examples:
   Scribner's Album of American History.
   Harper's Worldmark Encyclopedia of the Nations.

7. Books published by less well-known or smaller publishing houses. Following is a very brief lits of examples:

> Caxton Printers. Caldwell, Idaho.
> Golden Gate Press. San Francisco, California.
> Harvey House Publications. Irvington-on-Hudson, New York.
> Kenedy & Son. New York, N. Y.
> Oceana Publications. Dobbs Ferry, New York.

8. Publications of professional associations, societies, and foundations.
   Examples:
   > publications of National Geographic Society, National Education Association, Pan American Union, American Library Association, Boy Scouts of America, Y.W.C.A. and Y.M.C.A. (Association Press), UNESCO publications, American Association for the Advancement of Science.

9. Publications of museums.

10. Foreign imports

11. Publications of the U.S. Government
    These may be ordered directly from the Government Printing Office in Washington, D. C. if payment accompanies the order. If payment cannot be made in this manner, it is possible to buy through an agent who will pay for the materials at the time he buys them for you and you will be billed in this amount plus the agent's commission—usually about 15%.

12. State or county or local government publications.

13. Some companies sell only directly through their own offices or their agents. Examples of this type include the H. W. Wilson Company, Creative Educational Society, Spencer Press.

14. Titles which the jobber has not supplied from an order may be ordered from some other source.

15. Out of print books for which it is necessary to search may be ordered from a book seller who makes it part of his services to provide this special help. Large jobbers who handle many accounts frequently cannot provide the searching service. This is especially true if a time limitation is placed on the completion date.

For addresses of any company consult the list of publishers addresses in the *Children's Catalog* and in the *Basic Book List for Elementary School Libraries.* As you are using these addresses, it is well to remember that you should consider writing to each publisher, asking that your school or institution be put on a mailing list to receive all catalogs and announcements of their publications. This will be a great help in keeping the library files up-to-date with new publication lists.

Some jobbers are providing services other than merely supplying books. It is possible to order some titles from some jobbers with prepared catalog cards or with partially prepared catalog cards or with complete processing of the book except for accessioning. These companies do not, as a rule, give you as much discount as a jobber who provides only books. Obviously if you wish this extra service, it must be paid for.

It is also possible, in some parts of the United States, to buy books cooperatively with other institutions and to have processing services provided at an additional cost. It may prove very helpful to make inquiries of professional librarians in your area concerning such services.

Buying the Supplies

At the time when the book collection is being assembled and ordered, it will be necessary to give some thought to the supplies which will be needed to process this collection. If the ordering is done at this time, the supplies necessary to do the processing will probably be available when the books begin to come from the supplier.

Supplies which will be needed may be purchased from any of the companies specializing in distributing library supplies or, in some areas, from the local stationery stores. Or it may be that some of the supplies will be improvised and made from materials which can be available if money for the purchase of supplies is not.

You will need the following: 1. accession record (preferably a loose-leaf note book form), 2. book pockets, 3. date due slips, 4. book cards, 5. paste, 6. paste brushes, 7. ownership stamp, 8. pen and ink, or electric stylus and transfer paper, 9. catalog cards, 10. shellac or plastic spray. These are the minimums.

The quantity will depend upon the number of books which will form the library collection. Pockets, date due slips, book cards will be ordered in the same number as books in the collection, since most books will require one of each. The accession record sheets be ordered in quantity to supply one line for each title to be added to the collection. For these items allow about 5 cents per book for small collections, 4 cents per book for large collections. This difference is due to the discounted prices for large quantity ordering.

If you have enough money to buy printed catalog cards, they will cost about twelve cents per book. Instructions are given in the following chapter for ordering these cards. If you do not have enough money for printed cards, it will be essential to order blank cards, allowing for five cards per book, so that the catalog cards for the books may be typed. The cost for the blank cards will depend upon two factors— the number of cards you are buying and the quality of the paper in the cards. Costs may be from 3 cents to 5 cents for the cards for one book. An examination of the catalogs of the various supply companies will be helpful in working out your selections in terms of your budget.

Allow about 2 cents per book for the other supplies— paste, shellac, transfer paper, ink, brushes, stylus, etc. The prices, again, will vary depending upon what you choose to buy.

Over-all, from the least expensive processing to the most expensive, the costs will vary from about 5 cents to 15 cents per book for all supplies, and exclusive of the time of the workers.

Some of the better-known supply houses in the United States include:

Bro-Dart Industries:
  56 Earl Street, Newark 14, New Jersey.
  1888 South Sepulveda Boulevard, Los Angeles, California.
  520 King Street, West, Toronto 2B, Canada.

Demco Library Supplies:
  Box 852, Fresno, California.
  Box 4231 Hamden, Connecticut.
  Box 1488, Madison, Wisconsin.

Fordham Equipment Company:
  2377 Hoffman Street, New York 58, New York.

Gaylord Bros., Inc.:
  155 Gifford Street, Syracuse, New York.
  29 North Aurora Street, Stockton, California.

Library Bureau, Remington Rand Systems:
  122 East 42nd Street, New York 17, New York.
  984 Bay Street, Toronto 5, Canada.

Some of these companies, and others, too, may have offices in other major world cities. If your telephone directory does not help you, a note to the closest office of any of the above companies asking for assistance will be promptly answered.

Do not forget, either, your local stationery stores and any nearby professional librarians.

It would be well, before developing an order, to spend some time looking through the supply catalogs to note the different kinds of supplies, to see how they are described, and to see how this description fits into the actual work procedures. You will become aware, too, of the variations in prices as you buy more or less in quantity and as you select different styles of the various items. The guide post for you should be your budget and the size of the job.

You will also want to be sure, at this time, that you have ordered the basic reference materials which you will be using in processing the books. This list was included on page 6.

After you have decided what you will need to buy, you should check with the business department of the organization to see what form is used for ordering supplies. You will probably submit your list to the offices for ordering or prepare the orders yourself. If your particular institution does not have a set form, or if you are buying from moneys other than those of the institution, you may find it suitable to use the order form which some of the companies include in their catalogs.

Payment, of course, will have to be arranged on the basis of how your budget operates. You should have a clear understanding of whether or not you need to indicate the method of payment to the company at the time the order is sent.

As you read through the following chapters you will want to notice especially the descriptions of the supplies, how they are used, and the purposes they fulfill.

Keeping the Accounting Records

After the requisitions are typed and before they are sent to the business offices, the financial records should be set up. These, in the simplest form, consist of records to identify each requisition, the charges for the materials included in each requisition, and the balance which remains following the commitment of money for these materials. Here is an example which can be developed on regular office stationery or loose-leaf paper:

ACCOUNT OF: x x x x x Library   Allocation: $xxxx

Purchase Requisition

Date	Order No.	No.	Company	Amount	Balance	Paid
Jan. 2	631	1	John Smith	$16.00	$5084.	X
Jan. 2	632	2	Jobber	$1500.00	$3584.	1421.00
Jan. 2	635	3	Encyc. Co.	$139.00	$3445.	X
Jan. 2	634	4	Company 1	$94.00	$3351.	96.22
Jan. 2	633	5	Company 2	$621.00	$2730.	618.50

January 21 ADJUSTED BALANCE $2809.28

In the form above, each requisition has been entered, giving the information about it as the heading indicates. The column headed "Paid" refers to the actual amount for which the library is charged. It may reflect a difference in price due to incomplete orders or due to changes in the prices of book titles. At any rate, following the receipt of the orders, it is necessary to record the amount actually paid and to allow for any differences in total charges. In the example given, the charges were less than anticipated, so the balance which can be used for additional purchases is actually larger than anticipated. A record such as this will avoid overdrawing accounts. At no time should this be allowed.

Note also that when the amount charged is equal to the amount allowed, we do not find it necessary to repeat the sum, but use a symbol such as a check to indicate that the amounts are exactly alike.

4

Ordering Printed Catalog Cards

The Importance of Printed Catalog Cards

Chapters VIII and IX discuss the cataloging process, kinds of catalog cards, and the use of the card catalog at some length. By using the printed catalog cards the cataloging process is simplified, the various kinds of necessary cards for each book are provided, and the establishing of the card catalog may be accomplished more readily when printed cards are available than when they are not. The use of these prepared cards will save many, many hours of work in all of these processes. If the value of the time of the typists and of the catalogers and classifiers is estimated and compared with the number of hours involved in doing all the work as against doing only the completing of the printed cards, it will be found that it is less expensive to buy the printed cards and to use them than it is to do all the technical and clerical work oneself. Time is, after all, one of the most expensive assets we have. It is for this reason and this reason primarily that most established libraries try to make use of prepared cards.

There are two major sources for buying printed catalog cards for books published in the United States—the H. W. Wilson Company (950 University Avenue, New York 68, N. Y.) and the Library of Congress of the United States (Washington, D. C.) The buying procedures which are to be used differ for these two agencies, and these differences may help you decide where to do your buying. The choice of one kind of card or the other will also be dependent upon knowing what the differences in the handling of the cards is and what it means to the user.

Preparing the Book Order Cards or Work Cards for Catalog Card Orders

In order to prepare for the ordering of printed catalog cards it is necessary to use the book order cards which were developed for the new book orders and to use the work cards which were developed for the existing or inherited collection of books. These two sets of cards will have to be inter-filed. This filing is done so that the cards are arranged alphabetically by the authors' last names. If one author has several books listed, file the cards first by the author and within the author listing by title. Here is an example of a correct sequence:

Holt, S.
    Dictionary of American History.

last card in this group

Finkel, L. S. and Krawitz, R.
    How to study.

next to last card in this group

second card in this group

Coplan, Kate, and others.
    Poster ideas and bulletin board techniques.

first card in this group

Coplan, Kate
    Effective library exhibits.

The examples above are not complete work or order cards, but show the correct sequence of arrangement by author. All titles are titles from Oceana Publications.

Ordering Wilson Cards

The H. W. Wilson Company, among the many materials it provides for use in libraries, prints sets of catalog cards for many books published in the United States. These sets of cards sell for 12¢ each, making this the cost for each book's catalog cards. Each set will include the correct cards for the various ways the books should be listed in the card catalog. There will be an author card, a card for the title of the book, and as many subjects as have been chosen to describe the book for the user.

To buy these cards it is necessary to know which books have had cards made for them. Write to the H. W. Wilson Company and ask for their "Checklist of Catalog Cards". You should receive the necessary lists of titles promptly. Expect to receive, and look for in the materials you receive: one thickish pamphlet which covers the years 1938-1964; and monthly leaflets covering the 1965 publications to bring the lists up-to-date. For subsequent years there will be combinations of several years' lists, with the month-by-month lists to keep the lists current. Each of these lists, you will note, gives you instructions concerning which lists you need to use to supplement it.

An examination of these lists will show you that the books are listed by author, alphabetically by last name with only the initial letter of the given name. Then comes the titles, with the author's name repeated for each title if more than one title of one author appears. Notice that this is the way which we have just described for you on page 41, and that this is the form you will use in developing your order list.

Now, with the alphabetic-by-author file of cards and the checklists from the Wilson Company, you are ready to move to the next step. This work is easier to do if two or more people work together. It consists of reading the author's name, reading the title for each book from the card file and checking it against the entries in the checklist, aphabetically, to see if this author and this particular title are included. If the title is listed, put a small red check in front of the title or underline it in red—in the checklist. Use a hard lead pencil for this because, as you have noted, the print in the lists is very fine and a soft pencil may smudge over several titles. Also check the card in the upper right hand corner. This will provide you with a coding system so that you will know exactly which books you can expect to get cards for and which you will not be able to get cards for.

One word of caution must be included. If you have looked carefully at the envelope of materials which came to you from the Wilson Comany, you will have noted a special list of DISCONTINUED TITLES for which cards are no longer available. This means exactly what it says. So, if the title is listed in one of the catalogs, but also in this discontinued list, do not check either the checklist or the order cards (work card) for the title. It will be wasted effort.

After you have completed all the checking, count the number of titles for which you will be receiving books. There are several ways in which you can actually handle the requisitioning.

The first method is to place an order for as many "coupons" as you have titles to order. Each coupon costs 12¢ and is good for one set of catalog cards. These coupons can be used for any subsequent order and this is a useful way to have funds set aside in advance of the actual request for cards for particular titles.

If you order these coupons, you would receive from the company, upon their receipt of your purchase order, small sheets of paper, each with 25 coupons printed on it. These coupons will be returned to the company when a list of titles is submitted for which cards are requested.

Another way to handle the requisitions, and one to use when the institution is going to pay for the cards, is to submit a regular requisition form with a legend similar to this:

100 (or the correct quantity)	sets of catalog cards for titles as per the attached list at 12¢ per set	$12.00
	plus service charge	.12
		$12.12

Along with this kind of order you would send your red-checked list. This can be released since you have already coded your cards. If you have a great many titles use only this method.

A third method of ordering is one which is described in some of the material sent you by the Wilson company. If you will read the material closely, you will note that you are asked to copy authors and titles on small sheets of paper. This form is recommended when you do not have many titles to order cards for. When this method is used, coupons should accompany the order.

Note, also, that whenever you send in a list of titles for which you want the catalog cards, you should specify that you want the cards WITH CLASSIFICATION NUMBERS and WITH CATALOG HEADINGS.

Ordering Library of Congress Cards

There are also available for purchase printed cards which are prepared and sold by the Library of Congress of the United States. This means that two main sources for printed cards may be used.

Since 1871 the Library of Congress has been the legal depository for materials copyrighted in the United States. This does not mean that there is available a card for every book printed, but it does mean that cards are available for a very great number of books.

The method of ordering is a bit more complicated than that described for using to order Wilson cards. The format

Frick, Bertha Margaret, 1894-   ed.
025.33   Sears list of subject headings; with suggestions for the be-

SUBJECT HEADINGS

025.33   Sears list of subject headings; with suggestions for the be-
ginner in subject heading work. 8th ed. by Bertha Margaret Frick.   Wilson, H.W. 1959

025.33   Sears list of subject headings; with suggestions for the be-
ginner in subject heading work. 8th ed. by Bertha Margaret Frick.   Wilson, H.W. 1959
610p

First published 1923 as List of subject headings for small libraries,
by Minnie Earl Sears. The 1959 edition has been thoroughly revised and
brought up-to-date. This list follows the Library of Congress headings,
abridged to meet the needs of the smaller libraries. The classification
numbers have been assigned by the Decimal Classification Editorial Office
from the (8th) Abridged Dewey Decimal classifications

1 Subject headings   i Frick, Bertha Margaret, 1894-   ed.
025.33

59W5,529   ●   (W) The H. W. Wilson Company

**Catalog Cards with printed classification numbers and
with subject headings.**

025.33   Sears list of subject headings; with suggestions for the be-
ginner in subject heading work. 8th ed. by Bertha Margaret Frick.   Wilson, H.W. 1959
610p

1 Subject headings i Frick, Bertha Margaret, 1894-   ed.   025.33

59W5,529   ●   (W) The H. W. Wilson Company

Shelf List card for the above set.

of the cards, too, differs, but the information necessary for the catalog is included.

It is recommended that Wilson cards be considered first choice and that Library of Congress cards be ordered only when the Wilson Company cannot supply them for a large quantity of books. To order Library of Congress cards, you will need to write to: The Card Division, Library of Congress, Washington, D. C. Request the latest copy of its *Handbook of Card Distribution*. This will specify the exact method to be used, how payment is to be made, and a description of other special services.

The Library of Congress will send forms to use in ordering cards from its stock. You will need to fill in the information which is requested, using the information on your order (work) cards. One other item of information may be necessary. This is called the Library of Congress Number or the L.C. Number. It is a number assigned to the title at the time of publication and registry for copyright (by the Library of Congress). This number is made up of two parts and it will look something like this: 41-50212. This may be interpreted to mean that the particular book assigned this number was published and copyrighted in 1941 and that it was the 50,212th book which was granted a copyright in that year.

This number is found, for new titles, on the back of the title page. It may be included in a publisher's catalog of his titles. It is not included in the *Children's Catalog* or in the *A.L.A. Basic List*. There is a reference book which is used by librarians which does have these Library of Congress numbers listed, and you would probably find that most public libraries have it. It is called the *Cumulative Book Index* and it is published monthly (with 6 month and yearly accumulated editions). It lists all materials published in the United States and many published elsewhere if they are in English.

Library of Congress cards usually come without subject headings printed in and without classification numbers.

5

Receiving the Book Order

The Importance of Proper Receiving Procedures

Accounting for other people's money is always important. It is a mark of trust to be given the privilege of spending public moneys, as for a school system, and such trust always carries with it responsibilities. Anyone who is spending public money needs to be able at any time to show what it has purchased and to tell for what purpose it was spent.

It is also important for the individuals in charge of buying for a library to know how much has been spent, how much remains to be spent, what books have been received, and what has not been received. Proper handling of orders will also make it possible to know at any time what has not been ordered which needs to be ordered.

In performing these duties, you will see that there are several jobs involved and that these jobs may be organized in several ways. The clearing may be done "one at a time", handling each book as a unit. Or it may be preferable to use the "assembly line" method, doing one process for all books and then moving along to the second process, and so on. The method selected should take into consideration the number of people working, their skill, the amount of space available for working, the facilities.

Preparing for Unpacking Shipments

Opening and unpacking books may sound like the most menial of tasks, but even this process calls for some special handling. If your ordering procedures have called for or given any special coding to the orders themselves, it is well to know about these. Speak to the individual who actually places the orders to discover what these may be. One example of such special sequences is given in the following description.

After requisitions leave the hands of the library personnel, they probably go to some business department. That department may issue a form called a "purchase order" which is a legal form used to authorize the delivery of the goods listed on it and to make a legal committment to pay for the materials so ordered. Such forms may be coded by numbers or letters or combinations. There may be several such purchase order forms involved with a large order of books. Every "order direct" will have to have a separate authorization, and a "jobber's order" may be broken into several parts of a larger order to make it more convenient to handle smaller quantities. This coding will probably be reported to the person handling library orders and services so that the individual will know that the orders have been placed and will know what is included in each final order.

If such "purchase order" forms are received by you or given to you, examine them. Note how they are related to the original requisitions. Note, also, any coding which is used. Keep all these forms together, stapling the "purchase order" form to the requisition forms which they pertain to. For "order directs" it is advisable also to keep these forms in folders numerically or alphabetically, depending on which method pertains to the way in which the orders have been issued.

As packages or boxes of books begin to arrive, examine the outside of the box or package, with special attention to the label, to see if there is any identification of the books which are inside. Is there, for instance, a purchase order number given? Is there a requisition number given? Is the pubisher's name or the jobber's name given? Or are any of these clues given in combination with one another? In other words, try to match the books inside the box to the requisitions for them before you open the box.

It is possible that it was necessary to send several boxes of books to take care of the titles from one set of requisitions or one purchase order. This should be verified, if possible, before unpacking so that all books which are part of an order will be received together.

Having found the requisition (and its purchase order) for the group of books, the box or boxes may be opened. Be extremely careful in opening boxes of books. Usually they are packed very firmly together and the boxes are sealed very, very tightly. If a knife or sharp blade of some kind is used to open the box, care should be taken to avoid cutting any deeper than the sealing tape or the cardboard cover or the packing materials. It is easy to damage bindings by careless handling of knives.

Try this sequence: 1. Turn the box right-side up. 2. Cut the tape at the top edge, where the tape holds the cover to the body of the box. 3. The top should now be loose but not separate from the rest of the box. 4. Insert the fingers just under the top of the box. With the other hand feel for the indentation in the tape which marks the two edges of the top cover area. 5. Gently lift this top and with a blade score the tape at this indentation, cutting just through the tape. This will probably loosen the top so that it may be opened. Once the box is opened, remove the books carefully. Look for any packing slips, invoices or bills which accompany the shipment. These may be in an envelope which is clearly marked, they may be loose in the box, or they may be inserted in one of the books, or there may be none. Look carefully through any packing materials so that such forms are not discarded with the packing. If several boxes are involved with the one shipment, it is possible that only one packing slip, or invoice, is included and that it will cover the entire list of books.

Checking and Accounting for Titles in a Shipment

Unpacking books for a library consists of more than taking books out of boxes. You will need to have your purchase orders and requisitions which match the shipment. Check these against the packing slip or invoice found in the box to be certain that you have the correct requisition and purchase order for this group of books.

Begin, then, to unpack the books, checking each as it comes from the box to be sure that it is not damaged. As you do this, it will be helpful to stack the books in several piles (or, if you are so fortunate to have shelves, place them on the shelves) by publishers. This step may be omitted if only one publishers materials are included. But it will simplify the work later on if this separation job is done as the books are unpacked because this is the format used in typing the requisitions. This procedure will facilitate the double checking job to be done—matching the titles received to the requisitions and, at the same time, to the packing slips or invoice forms.

Examine the invoice to see if the book titles are arranged by publisher or by author or by title or without any order.

Begin to check each title against the listing in the requisition and against the invoice. Place a √ before the title on each form as each book is cleared. Pay attention at this point to the number of copies ordered or to the number of volumes in a set. Be sure you receive what you order. If there are differences in the titles requested and those sent, set aside such problems. Occasionally titles are confused by those who are handling the preparation of the shipment, and such errors will be reported later.

Verify at this time that the price is correct. If the invoice or packing slip does not give a price, there is nothing you can do about it now. If the price is included, compare it with the price on the requsition. When they are not the same, check the book, itself, to see if the dust jacket has a price printed on it. This may be a new list price and may or may not be that which has been quoted on the invoice or packing slip. It is possible that the price of the book has changed several times between the time that it was entered on the list from which you selected it and that time when the jobber packed the book to fill your order. Should the price, however, be completely out of line, make a note on the requisition in red pencil to establish the price charged. This will be necessary for accounting purposes.

Look, next, in the file of the order cards for the one covering this title. If the card indicates that a printed set of catalog cards has been ordered, remove the order card and check in the boxes of Wilson cards or Library of Congress cards for the packet of cards for the book. Put all cards for the book inside the book. If there are no printed cards available, the order card only will be placed in the book. It is to become the word card for the book and will remain with the book until all its processing has been completed. Books with the prepared cards may be housed, now, in one area—in shelves or in boxes—and books without the prepared cards should be placed in a separate area.

Continue this processing for all books received. When the checking of the order has been completed, and when the order has been filled correctly, all the business forms should be returned to the business department, reporting that the order has been filled correctly.

When the order is incomplete, check to see if there is still time for additional shipments to be received before the closing date for filling the order. If there is additional time, hold the requisitions, the invoice and purchase orders together until the closing date. As additional parts of the order are delivered, handle them as described above.

At the time that the report goes to the business office to

clear for payment any damaged books and any imperfect books should be reported. These can be replaced without charge. The commonest types of imperfections to notice include: 1. the wrong cover bound to the book. 2. covers attached up-side-down. 3. Sections of the book missing. 3. damage to cover or contents such as machine cuts or extensive soilage.

There is one other job to be done at this time—clearing and correcting the running account in the charges against the budget. You will want to refer to the account form and the example given on page 38. It is at this time that we can add the adjustment figures. Remember that the payment column will now include the amount actually charged for the books including any postal charges. If only a part of the shipment has arrived, make such a note and attach it to the account page so that further additions and adjustments may be made.

6

Processing The Books

The Accession Record

The accession record is a list of all the titles belonging to the library, given in the order in which they have been added, day by day. This is a numerical list, with a single number being assigned to each title in a correct numerical sequence. No two books have the same number. The first book is assigned number 1; the second book becomes number 2; the third is number 3, and so on.

The accession record is also a permanent record of what has been added to the library, when it was added, and any statement concerning the loss, transfer, or discard of a title. In this way it becomes a sort of history of the collection, telling what happened to each of the books ever purchased for it.

All books are accessioned. The information included in this listing has become fairly uniform so that most accession records include these items: the author, the title; the publisher; the year of publication; the cost of the book; where the book came from; who paid for it; the volume number (if part of a set); the copy number (if there are several copies of the book in the library); and the disposition of the book. Many libraries add other information such as dates of rebinding.

You will note the sample page given below. This is a typical type of accession record. Such printed forms can be purchased from regular library supply houses, both in bound and in loose-leaf form. The loose-leaf form may be equipped with a hard cover of the appropriate size. For most libraries, the loose-leaf form is more desirable since this makes it possible to type the information on the pages and to make revisions should these be necessary. The permanently bound form is less flexible and requires that all entries be hand written.

Some libraries, usually those with extensive collections and those which are not apt to be open to public inquiry, have eliminated such records and keep only a shelf list for their inventory of books and for any record of holdings. Chapter X treats of the shelf list and discusses its function in detail. At this time it is important only to note that for small libraries and for libraries which need to have a permanent record of what they have owned and what has happened to it, the accession record is indispensable.

If you do not have money to buy standard supplies, you can make your own accession record forms by using typing paper or notebook paper purchased in bulk and punched with two, three, or four holes to fit standard loose-leaf binders. Use the sample form given, allowing about 25 titles to each page. Check to see if mimeograph services are available and arrange to have this form copied on a stencil. Several hundred sheets can be run through the mimeograph machine in a matter of minutes, giving you a future supply.

Date	No.	Author	Title	Pub.	Year	Source	Cost	Remarks
9/64	01	Butler, Roger	Let's build a cabin	x x	x x	Gift	Free	c.1
	02	Morley,Clare	Pacific Pirates	x x	1961	"	"	c.1
	03	"	"	"	"	Bd. Ed.	1.20	c.2
	04		xxxxx Encyclopedia	x x	1963	"	98.00	v.1
	05		"	"	"	"	Per	v.2
	06		"	"	"	"	set	v.3
	07		"	"	"	"		v.4
	08		"	"	"	"		v.5
	09		"	"	"	"		v.6
	10		"	"	"	"		v.7
	11		"	"	"	"		v.8

Or it may be a hand-lettered notice which reads:

Or it may be a notation typed on a gummed label such as is available at any stationery store, using the same legend as above.

The important need is to have the instructions in the book. These are usually pasted in or written in the book on the lining paper of the back cover—centered at the top for the sake of appearance and uniformity.

Reference books do not need pockets or date due slips or bookcards. These will be mentioned later, and it is important to know that this group of books is excluded from these steps in library processing.

Date Due Slips

The date due slip is a simple device for helping the borrower of books keep track of when he needs to return them to the library. Many large libraries use other methods for providing this information to its borrowers, but this is one of the simplest ways to make the information available.

The slip may be a printed, a mimeographed, or unmarked piece of thin paper, of a convenient size. Three inches by five inches is one of the standard sizes.

This slip should be pasted on the lining paper at the back of the book—on the page opposite the hard cover. It should be pasted flush with the top of this lining paper and it should be centered across the page. Very little paste should be used, preferably one thin line across the top of the date due slip with the paste brush.

Although this may seem overly particular for such a small item, it, too, has a purpose behind it. Eventually it will be necessary to replace the slip. When that time comes, it is simple to pull this loose slip upwards and off of the lining paper without tearing into the body of the page. Another slip can be placed directly over the spot left by the one removed.

Book Pockets

Book pockets are small envelope-like forms or paper supports to hold a book card (see next section of this chapter). They are pasted in the book, usually on the lining of one of the covers, front or back. They are also, usually, pasted near the bottom of the lining and are centered—this placement will result in a neat and attractive looking page.

It is recommended that book pockets be pasted inside the back cover, centering them and aligning them with the bottom edge of the lining papers. This, too, is functional. First, it keeps the "business" of circulation out of sight. Second, when a pocket is torn or soiled or needs replacement, there will be little damage to the lining page if the old pocket is ripped out with a downward motion. The tearing of the lining paper at the lower edge is usually the only damage noticeable. By pasting the fresh pocket over this area, the damage will be repaired.

In some books the end papers are attractively decorated by maps or other illustrations which add materially to the interest in the book. Sometimes, too, there are illustrated end papers, both front and back, and these are different. In such cases as this, do not paste pockets or date due slips here. Instead, move them one page inside the book, pasting both the pocket and the date due slip on the inside of the last lining paper.

There is one other case when you do not put the pocket on the inside of the back cover. That is when there is going to be a plastic cover put over the dust cover of the book. In that case, put the pocket (and the date due slips) on the back, left, lining paper. If it should interfere with the plastic cover, it can be moved inside.

Book Cards

Book cards are used for circulation purposes. They are, for small libraries, one of the simple and inexpensive ways of keeping track of who has borrowed what book. When a book is to be borrowed from the library, the borrower signs his name on the book card, adding any other information considered pertinent by the library. The card is then left in the library and put into a file of other cards representing books in circulation. When the book is returned, the card is taken from the borrowers file and returned to the book to be used for the next circulation.

Large libraries will probably use electronic methods for keeping circulation records and they will, probably, not use book cards or will use them in some other way. However, for the small library, this method permits the library to have the records it needs.

To be useful, the book card must have enough information on it to identify the book it stands for. It must have the author and the title, of course. To further identify it, there should be the call number (to be discussed in chapter seven) and the accession number.

In actually setting up the work sequence for processing the books, it is possible to type, in part, the information to go on the book cards before the books have been received or any recording of information is made. The cards could not, of course, be complete, but the author and title can be typed on them early in this work and the classification number and accession number can be added later. If this is done, the book card should then accompany the "order card" or "work card".

After the card is typed, it is placed in the pocket of the book where it stays except when the book is in circulation. At that time, it provides the library with the information necessary covering its disposition.

Identification Marks

All books should be marked with an ownership statement of some kind which is difficult to erase. These serve as permanent and distinctive identification for the materials which are a part of any library's collection.

The least expensive form is probably to write or letter the information for identification in the book, but handwriting or hand lettering for this purpose is awkward since it can be imitated or erased.

The next least expensive method of marking the materials is to use a rubber stamp made especially for the particular library. These are not at all expensive and, used with indelible ink pads, are very satisfactory. They may be quickly

641 S		893
Scheib, Ida		
AUTHOR		
First book of food		
TITLE		

DATE DUE	BORROWER'S NAME	ROOM NUMBER

DEMCO 239

BOOK CARD

made at most stationery stores or may be purchased from one of the library supply houses. In using these, consider establishing a wording which gives the name of the library, the parent institution if there is one, and the place.

EXAMPLE:

Emerson Junior High School
Board of Education
Yonkers, N. Y.

An example of what not to do follows:

POOR EXAMPLE:

Emerson Elementary School Library
Board of Education
Yonkers, N. Y.

Instead of using two name forms which are as similar as these, even though the information is correct, it would be much better to use the following for the elementary school's library:

BETTER EXAMPLE:

Elementary Library—Emerson School
Board of Education
Yonkers, N. Y.

The reason, of course, is obvious. There is a quicker identification when the initial words are different and when the reader does not have to become involved with looking for one different word.

Note that in each case the first line identifies the library; the second line identifies the parent institution; the third line identifies the geographical location.

If desired, other information such as street and number, insignia, symbols, etc. can all be part of the ownership stamp.

A more expensive way of identifying the owner, and a way more necessary for large institutions is the embossing of the insignia. This is done by using a metal stamp. In its simplest form it resembles a pair of pliers or scissors or tongs with embossing plates opposite the handles instead of the grasping area of the pliers or tongs or the cutting edges of scissors. These ends look like huge coins. One of these plates is incised, the other is raised, with the same insignia, so that when the two fit together, under pressure on the handles, these two plates come together. The paper is between them and it is pushed up into the incised form by the raised form. This embossing form is used on many legal documents for identification because it is almost impossible to remove it.

Embossing equipment can also be heavier and more elaborate or it may even be operated by electric power. Such heavier equipment is used for those libraries and institutions with extensive quantities of materials and with the funds necessary to provide the equipment.

Regardless of the kind of ownership mark to be used, it should be placed inside the book in several places, all for safeguarding the identification of the owners. Typical places are 1. on the book pocket (when the book pockets are not printed with the name of the institution); 2. on the title page of the book; 3. on the first page of the text. One other page may prove to be a desirable addition—namely, a "secret page"—a page somewhere within the book whose use will be known only to the librarian. This page can be used for other kinds of identification, too, such as the accession number.

Marking the Spine With and Without Plastic Covers

The last step in the physical processing of the book is the transferring of the call number of the book to the outside of the spine. Having this number (made up of the classification number and the author's initial, and discussed in chapter seven) on the spine permits these numbers to be seen when the book is on the shelf. It becomes easier for the user to identify the subject of the book and it assists both the reader and the librarian in shelving the book correctly.

If the library does not have money for plastic covers to place over the dust jackets, the process is very simple. The dust jacket is removed and the number is written directly on the spine. In order to keep these numbers of more or less uniform size and to have them in about the same place on the backs of all books, make a marking guide. Use a piece of cardboard about four to five inches long. Measure a distance three inches from the bottom of the card and another distance two inches from the bottom of the card. Draw lines across the card at each of these points. Notice that there is a one-inch space between the lines. Then, using a sharp knife or a very sharp scissors, cut along each of these lines a distance of about two inches from one side. Make, also, a cut at this point from the top line to the bottom line. This will remove a rectangle of cardboard from the original card, giving a notch which can be used for a distance guide in marking the books.

To use the guide, place it against the spine of the book, with the lower edge of the card at the lower edge of the spine. Using a pencil, draw a line at the top and at the bottom edges of the notch, horizontally across the spine of the book. In this space—a one-inch high area—it is possible to write the call letters of the book.

To do the numbering you may select from several kinds of tools and inks, depending upon your own skill in using them. The goal is to have the numbers and letters neat, readable, and as near like printing as possible. The following descriptions may help you select what you think will let you do the best job.

> Type 1: Permanent inks, available in black or dark blue and white. You will need both a dark and a light color, to use on bindings which will provide contrast and let the lettering stand out. Apply these liquid inks with a pen or brush, whichever you are most skilled in using.

> Type 2: Use an electric pencil and inked tape which is especially prepared to use with it. The electric pencil is similar to the "burning pencil" used in craft work. Called an electric stylus, these are equipped with wiring and plug in cords. As they are connected to electric power, they heat—the metal point heats. When it is hot it can be used with special inked tape to transfer the ink from the tape to the spine of the book.

Hold the tape firmly, dull side against the book, in the area you have marked on the spine. The heated point of the pencil traces the numbers on the shiny side of the tape. When the pencil is lifted, the marking remains.

Type 3: A special type of pen, similar to a fountain pen, requiring an "acetate ink." The ink is indelible. It is available in either dark or light colors. Lettering is done directly on the spine of the book, using the pen as if it were an ordinary one.

Type 4: You may buy special gummed labels from a library supply house. These are made of paper and have a permanent type glue. Type the call number on the label, remove the label from its backing and fix it to the spine of the book in the proper place.

With any of these four kinds of materials, it is helpful to add a protective coat of clear shellac over the entire spine after the ink has set. This will help keep the letters from chipping or wearing off. You may use either a clear shellac, applied with a brush or as a spray, or you may use one of the plastic sprays now available on the market.

If you are fortunate enough to have money to buy plastic covers for your library books, you will first need to fit the plastic covers over the dust jackets. Direction for attaching the covers usually come with the covers, and it is highly advisable to read them carefully and to follow the step by step description. In case you have "inherited" covers but no directions, the following may be helpful.

Plastic covers serve several purposes: they make it possible to continue to use the dust jacket and to let its attractive cover help "sell the book" to the user; they protect the book against soil damage; they help protect the cover against weather hazards; they help make the shelves look bright and attractive.

To place the call number on the plastic covers it is necessary to use the gummed labels. Most plastic will take only special kinds of ink. Heat is not to be used. So the gummed label is best. When plastic covers are used, it is well to place the pre-gummed label on the dust jacket rather than on the plastic cover. This method will allow the plastic cover to protect the call number label as well as the book's cover.

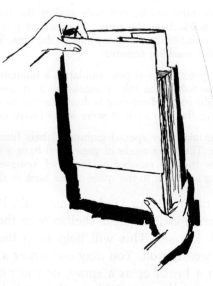

Select a plastic jacket which is the correct size for the dust jacket of
the book. The plastic jacket should permit the dust jacket to slip between its folds firmly so that there is no slippage.

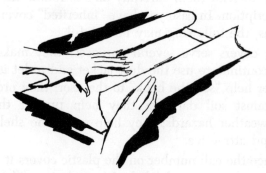

Lay the dust jacket against the clear surface of the plastic jacket. Any
folds or any opaque paper (part of the plastic cover) should lie against
the inside of the dust jacket. This permits the picture on the dust
jacket to remain as the cover of the book.

When using plastic covers which must be adjusted to fit the correct size of the dust jacket, fold over any of the excess length of material. Press such folds firmly, using a ruler or bone folder.

Wrap the now-covered jacket around the book, being sure to get the cover on right-side-up and front-to-front. Again, press the folds firmly.

Fasten the jacket to the book. For a permanent mounting, spread paste along the lining of the book at the point where the wrap-around cover ends. For a removable mounting, use transparent gummed tape at the top and bottom of the front and back covers, attaching the tape only to the plastic covers or to the plastic and dust covers.

SKETCHES HAVE BEEN PROVIDED BY
BRO-DART INDUSTRIES.

7

Classifying Books

How Classification Organizes a Collection

If you go back into history several hundred years, it is interesting to think about how collections of books—in whatever form the "book" happened to be at that time and in that place—were taken care of. Collections of books existed from remarkably early times in man's history, but not as we know them today. And most of the early collections of materials had limited use. Borrowers did not really borrow books. They could use the materials, but usually had to use them wherever they were housed. Many large libraries today still operate with some similar restrictions.

For libraries of this type—those to which the public, generally, does not have access and to whose collection only the trained librarian has access—almost any method of organizing the books for us is acceptable. And in the past the method of organizing was to put like materials together. It is an interesting set of "likenesses" which can be found through the ages. Books have been shelved by authors' names, by titles, by size, by accession numbers, by format, even by color.

Many libraries, early in their development, worked out their own systems and are still using systems developed several hundreds of years ago. These may have been extended, changed, refined and adapted, but in many countries the classification systems are known only to the staff of the library.

Numbering systems for library collections can be traced as far back as the 1580's—before there was a United States. And it was not until 1876 that the method which is now used so widely through the western world was developed.

And yet all systems had basically the same goals. It was necessary to know what was in the collection. It was important to have similar items together for subject identification or for individual identification. It was important to have the materials available—someone needed to be able to get easily what was needed.

The system which is used so widely today is a system which does all that and more.

The Dewey Decimal Classification System

Mr. Melvil Dewey was a remarkable man. He had many interests, but one which has changed the library world was his great concern about making libraries more orderly places. In 1876 he published, anonymously, an organizational pattern for systematizing library materials under the title of "A Classification and Subject Index for Cataloguing and Arranging the Books and Pamphlets of a Library." This came after he had worked out his ideas, tried them, reorganized them, polished them into a more workable form. This, with modifications and additions, is still the basis for what we call, more informally, the Dewey Decimal Classification System.

Mr. Dewey drew from several sources for his ideas and the name which he finally resolved for the system tells something about it. It is based upon the Arabic decimal system and the system is analytical by subject.

All the areas of man's knowledge were divided into ten main groups. These groups Mr. Dewey numbered by hundreds, beginning with a group for numbers less than 100.

But to keep the system uniform, these numbers, from 1 through 99, were prefixed with zeros in front of each to give the number three digits. So it is that we have numbers like 001, 009, 016, and so on to 099. The "zero hundred" group, then is the first group in the sequence. The second major group is 100. Then, in numerical sequence, come 200, 300, 400, 500, 600, 700, 800, and 900. And to each of these major divisions he assigned a subject.

The numbers from 000 through 099 include all materials which are general in subject rather than specifically limited to one area only. A good example of this is the number 030 which applies to encyclopedias—books which contain information about many, many topics. Also in this 000 group, may be found the number 070 which, like encyclopedias, allows for information on many subjects and refers to newspapers.

The 100 through 199 group includes all materials about philosophy. Philosophy is concerned with man's thoughts about himself, his place in life, and his responsibility in the universe. Two excellent examples of numbers in the 100 group which are used frequently in school materials are the numbers 150 and 170. Dealing with behavior of people, describing acceptable behavior in our society as well as how man has behaved in other societies, number 150 interprets man's thoughts about himself and his relation to other people. Here, too, is the number for books about manners for young people, because manners have to do with what is acceptable in society. Such a problem as ethics, that is, what is right and what is wrong, will belong here.

The other number mentioned, 170, is used for books on psychology—how man thinks, what makes him think and feel and behave as he does.

The 200 through 229 group deals with religion—religions of all people of all historical times. Good examples of what might be found in a school library include books describing the various religions and various religious documents. One very interesting subject included here treats of the myths and legends of the various countries of the world—the Norse legends of their gods, the Greek and Roman myths, the Hindu, Arabic, African, Aztec, and Mayan myths. All these represent what was, at one time, the religion of the various peoples. Here, too, would be the more modern religions of the Buddhists, the Confucian faith, the Judaic beliefs, the Christian doctrines. All religions of all times will be placed in this category.

In the next group, 300 through 399, there are placed those books which deal with anything pertaining to man's living in a society of men. Subjects such as government, and all its structures, education, political systems and political relations of countries, population problems, and problems of society are all a part of this group. For school libraries, and especially for libraries for young people, it is worth noting that here, too, are the fairy tales. They are here because they developed out of the past, came to each generation by word of mouth, and remain a part of the history of man's cultural development.

The 400 through 499 group is concerned with language— the history and meaning and use of all languages. Probably the best known books to be included here are the dictionaries of languages, all languages—English, Spanish, German, French, Dutch, Portuguese. These are some of the European languages. But languages of all peoples belong here, too. Igbo, Urdu, Hindi, dialects from Vietnam and from Siberia, from the Polynesian Islands to Iceland—the languages of all the world find their way to one spot. They all belong here.

If this numbering begins to sound very set and dry, the next grouping should change that belief. Knowledge in every area today is expanding very quickly. But knowledge in science, in particular, has been most dramatic and most spectacular. The numbers 500 through 599 are for science, and this grouping has had expansion and adjustments to take care of and to accommodate the new information man has gathered. It is particularly worthy of noting that Mr. Dewey's system has been flexible enough to accommodate this tremendous expansion as well as the more traditional aspects of the sciences. For this is the number group for all the natural sciences—mathematics, astronomy, chemistry, physics, geology, biology, botany, zoology, and paleontology.

Closely related to the science group is the 600 group. Materials which would be numbered within the 600 through 699 sequence must be concerned with the applications of science so that they become useful arts. The two expressions are, both, applied to the group. Let us look at several examples to see how we may interpret them correctly. If, in science, we discover a "theory of relativity", it is, truly, science and is given a 500 number. Then man takes that knowledge and splits an atom and it is still science, still 500. But he then takes that knowledge and builds an atomic powered submarine. That is the point at which he has applied his science to make something useful and it becomes a subject in the 600 group. In other words, when the pure scientific knowledge is applied to something, this becomes the materials which will go into the 600 grouping. Medicine is another example of the application of knowledge in science to a practical use. Apply the knowledge of mathematics to engineering and the knowledge and theories of force and energy to it, and there are further examples of the information included in the 600 group.

The 700 through 799 group contains all materials on fine arts—music, painting, drawing, sculpture, architecture, the theatre and dance. Here too, and with a fine distinction, are the materials on recreations. It is very interesting to see that Mr. Dewey regarded the skills of sports and athletics, of games and amusement as fine arts.

In the 800 through 899 section are the books of literature. Like language, this group represents all the literature of all the cultures of the world. Here are the plays, poetry,

74 HOW TO ORGANIZE A CHILDREN'S LIBRARY

essays, humor, and literary criticism of all ages. And here is where books of fiction—stories—belong. For convenience, however, we do not always place fiction in this category. This will be explained more in detail later on, but it is important in understanding the complete system, to know that those subjects we give special treatment to actually do belong within the system.

The 900 through 999 division is a very interesting one. It deals with history. But it treats of three separate and distinct kinds of history. From 930-999 the history is by world area and usually by historical periods within these areas. Not all history, however, is political, There is, also, a kind of history which describes the people and their life and customs. That, too, is here, in the 910 through 919 group. One further kind of history, more unusual as history than the others described, is the book which is the history of a person, or, as we say, biography. Books which treat of the lives of individuals are called "individual biography" and books which treat of the lives of several people are called "collective biographies". Both types are a part of the 900 group.

Many libraries, to simplify the organization and use of the 900 collections, however, classify the biographies, especially the individual biographies, in a different manner. This will be discussed later.

Let us, now that we have explained the major divisions, summarize them.

SUMMARY

000-099	General Works	600-699	Applied Science
100-199	Philosophy	700-799	Fine Arts
200-299	Religion	800-899	Literature
300-399	Sociology	900-999	History
400-499	Language (Philology)	Special Classification: Fiction	
500-599	Natural Science	Special Classification: Biography	

In order to further explain the classification system, it is necessary to show more detail of its workings. Let us, as an example, take the 500-599 group, natural science. As you noted earlier, there are many different sciences. To each of these is assigned a special number group. This second division of the numbered groups is by 10's. Within the 500 group there would be, then:

500-509 Books about science in general
510-519 Mathematics: all levels, all kinds of mathematical systems
520-529 Astronomy: beyond the earth, all universes
530-539 Physics: energy in all its forms
540-549 Chemistry: the elements of the earth
550-559 Geology: Earth sciences
560-569 Paleontology: prehistoric plant and animal life
570-579 Natural History and Nature Study
580-589 Botany: plant life
590-599 Zoology: animal life.

And each of these groups is, again, subdivided. Here is the example of the 510 group:

510 Mathematics in general
511 Arithmetic
512 Algebra
513 Geometry
514 Trigonometry
515 Descriptive Geometry
516 Analytical Geometry
517 Calculus
518 Special Functions
519 Probabilities.

And even this subdivision is not the last. Mr. Dewey also made use of the decimal point to show the relation of smaller parts of a subject to a more general subject. Arithmetic, which we tend to take for granted, has many parts, and the use of this system shows us some of them.

511.1   Number systems
511.2   Fundamental arithmetic operations
511.3   Prime numbers and factoring
511.4   Fractions and decimal fractions
511.5   Permutations and combinations
511.6   Proportion and ratio
511.7   Square and cube roots, exponents, and logs
511.8   Business arithmetic
511.9   Arithmetic problems
511.98 Arithmetic tables

It is interesting to note that mathematics as we learned it is no longer the same today. We are more aware of the various kinds of systems for handling measurement and for indicating the relations of quantities. If you have kept up-to-date, you are aware that what young people are learning in schools today is called "new mathematics". This term is used very loosely by many people. It may be helpful to note that Mr. Dewey anticipated and prepared for the inclusion of new knowledge which was to come even though he did not, specifically, know just what this knowledge would be.

One such example is that represented by the subject of "space flight" which was, in Mr. Dewey's day, an unknown area. This fits very nicely, however, into engineering (620) and 629, other branches of engineering. And then, eventually, into 629.4, aeronautics and space flight.

This analysis is given to let you see that the orderliness behind the system and its completeness do not rule out its flexibility. As you work with the system and as you begin to see how subjects fit into it, you will not only feel more at ease with it, but you will also develop a deep appreciation of the skill which went into Mr. Dewey's contribution to library organization.

Determining the Subject of the Book

Determining the subject of the book is the heart of the classification process. It is this decision which really makes it possible to bring together on the shelves those books which are about the same subject. It is not always an easy matter to determine what a book is about. Titles are very frequently misleading and the descriptions of books printed on their dust jackets may present so vivid a picture that you may want to read the book immediately, but the picture may have little to do with the real book. The most accurate method is, of course, to read the book and to relate it to known subject fields. Since it is impossible to do this, we must try to develop other methods which are both practical and briefer. A few general suggestions can be given, and as these are used and tested, book by book, skills can be developed in knowing how to approach special kinds of problems.

It is important at this time to refer to the following tools, and you will find it helpful to have them available:

1. Printed catalog cards. (We will refer both to the Wilson cards and the Library of Congress cards. Use those which you have or note the examples given.)
2. *The Children's Catalog.* 1961 ed.
3. *Dewey Decimal Classification Guide.* (either the abridged or unabridged edition)
4. *Basic Book Collection for Elementary Grades.*

In addition to these references, as you are actually working with a book to determine its subject, and hence its classification, you will refer to the book, itself, the dust jacket of the book, and, just possibly, a dictionary.

A. *When there are printed catalog cards available*

If either Wilson cards or Library of Congress cards are available for the book, there is no difficulty in classifying the book, for the work has already been done. Examine the card below, a typical Wilson Card, and you will note in the lower right-hand corner a number—641. This is the classification number from the Dewey Decimal Classication System which is appropriate for this book. You will note, also, that this number is printed in the upper left-hand corner of the card. (The number appears in this place only when request is made at the time the cards are ordered from the Wilson Company.)

If there are two numbers given, as in the next example, the following steps should be taken: 1. Using the *Children's Catalog*, the alphabetic listing, check to see if this title is included. If it is, look to the right of the entry in the list. There, in bold faced type, is a classification number. If it is one of those on the card, use it. 2. If the title is in-

641   **Scheib, Ida**
       First book of food: written and illus. by Ida Scheib.
Watts, F. 1956
       65p illus
          Map on lining-papers
          "Story of food before it reaches the neighborhood stores; how it is
grown or made, and the history of some of the things we eat. Included
are sections on cattle raising, dairy farming, poultry raising, truck
farming, wheat farming, flour milling, and baking, fruit raising, fishing,
and the production of other food commodities." Publisher's note
          About the author: p64

   1   Food   I Title   j641

60W8,989   ⬤   (W)   The H. W. Wilson Company

Typical Wilson Catalog Card with one classification number.

980   **Shepherd, William Robert**
       Hispanic nations of the New world; a chronicle of our
southern neighbors.   Yale Univ. Press 1919
       251p front maps (Chronicles of America ser. v50)

          Partial contents: Heritage from Spain and Portugal; Age of the
dictators; Peril from abroad; Mexico in revolution; Republics of the
Caribbean; Pan-Americanism and the great war; Bibliographical note

   1   Latin America—History   I Title   II Series   980 or 973

62W16,760   ⬤   (W)   The H. W. Wilson Company

Typical Wilson Catalog Card with two classification numbers.

cluded, but the number differs from that given on the Wilson card, look in the numbered listing for the description of the contents and for the name at the beginning of the section of this numbered group. If the description seems to go with the subject, use that number. 3. If the title is not listed, use the number on the card to find the section in the *Children's Catalog* for that number and compare the descriptions of books listed here with the description found on the dust jacket of the book we are working with. Also check the table of contents of the book, the preface and introduction and, if necessary, skim the first chapter to see how the book compares with the description for the books listed in *Children's Catalog*. If they seem to be similar, use the one number given for the one group of books which seems most similar to the book in hand. Remember, either of the numbers may be used correctly, but that a choice must be made.

There are, also, several types of books which will require that a decision be made to place them in special categories and to use this category for similar materials. One of the typical examples of this arises with books which treat of various vocations or of different kinds of work. All of these books which describe the education and special training of those who wish to enter the various professions or semi-skilled professions or trades used to be classified in the 300 group. They may, also, be classified under the particular subject which represents the area of work with which the job is concerned. For example, the next card is concerned with the education and training necessary to become a nurse. It may, correctly, be classified under either 610 (medicine) or under 371.42 (education for work). This last number will be found in most of the older collections of books, but is still preferred by some school libraries today.

A choice must be made for new libraries, however, and it will be helpful to think, in this case as in other cases, of the way in which the boys and girls using the collection will seek out materials. If the library is one of the services pro-

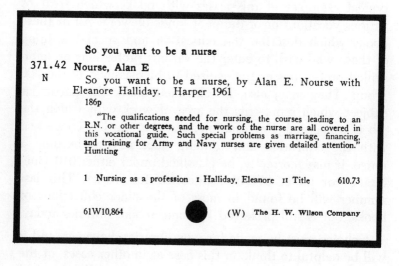

371.42 **Nourse, Alan E**
N
    So you want to be a nurse, by Alan E. Nourse with
Eleanore Halliday. Harper 1961
186p

    "The qualifications needed for nursing, the courses leading to an
R.N. or other degrees, and the work of the nurse are all covered in
this vocational guide. Such special problems as marriage, financing,
and training for Army and Navy nurses are given detailed attention."
Huntting

1 Nursing as a profession ı Halliday, Eleanore ıı Title   610.73

61W10,864   (W) The H. W. Wilson Company

    So you want to be a nurse
371.42 **Nourse, Alan E**
N
    So you want to be a nurse, by Alan E. Nourse with
Eleanore Halliday. Harper 1961
186p

    "The qualifications needed for nursing, the courses leading to an
R.N. or other degrees, and the work of the nurse are all covered in
this vocational guide. Such special problems as marriage, financing,
and training for Army and Navy nurses are given detailed attention."
Huntting

1 Nursing as a profession ı Halliday, Eleanore ıı Title   610.73

61W10,864   (W) The H. W. Wilson Company

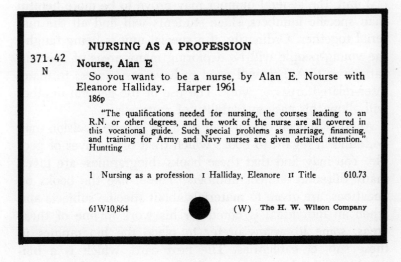

Halliday, Eleanore

371.42
N

Nourse, Alan E

So you want to be a nurse, by Alan E. Nourse with
Eleanore Halliday. Harper 1961
186p

"The qualifications needed for nursing, the courses leading to an
R.N. or other degrees, and the work of the nurse are all covered in
this vocational guide. Such special problems as marriage, financing,
and training for Army and Navy nurses are given detailed attention."
Huntting

1 Nursing as a profession   i Halliday, Eleanore   ii Title   610.73

61W10,864   (W)   The H. W. Wilson Company

NURSING AS A PROFESSION

371.42
N

Nourse, Alan E

So you want to be a nurse, by Alan E. Nourse with
Eleanore Halliday. Harper 1961
186p

"The qualifications needed for nursing, the courses leading to an
R.N. or other degrees, and the work of the nurse are all covered in
this vocational guide. Such special problems as marriage, financing,
and training for Army and Navy nurses are given detailed attention."
Huntting

1 Nursing as a profession   i Halliday, Eleanore   ii Title   610.73

61W10,864   (W)   The H. W. Wilson Company

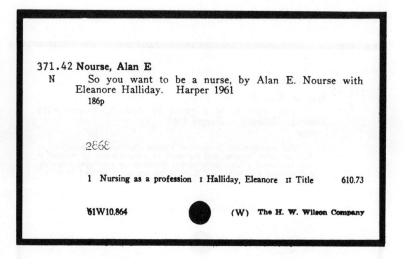

371.42 Nourse, Alan E
N   So you want to be a nurse, by Alan E. Nourse with
         Eleanore Halliday.   Harper 1961
         186p

         2868

         1 Nursing as a profession ɪ Halliday, Eleanore ɪɪ Title   610.73

         ʼ61W10.864   ●   (W)   The H. W. Wilson Company

vided by a school, it may be helpful to learn whether or
not the curriculum includes special units on vocations in
any of the grades served by this collection. If there is a special unit, the general number may prove to be more helpful
than specific numbers, since students will find all the material together. Ordinarily, if a special unit is being taught,
the young people will be exploring many areas of speciali-
zations so that they will need to have easy access to many
inter-related areas of work. The use of the general number
will allow this easy availability of materials.

Another special case which requires a basic decision may
be found in regard to books which treat of the lives of people. You may find that these books—biographies—are given
many different subject numbers. These, like the books on
vocations, are given to materials about specific subjects and
when an individual is noted for his work in one of these
areas, some librarians prefer to place the biographies in
these subject categories. The next card, which is a biography of the famous baseball player, may be classified as
either biography or baseball. It is recommended, however,

Silverman, Al
   Mickey Mantle: Mister Yankee. Putnam 1963
224p illus

"The life of the popular Yankee slugger whose baseball career has been one of the most exciting and interesting events in recent sports history." Bk Buyer's Guide

1 Baseball 2 Mantle, Mickey Charles   92

63W11,871   (W) The H. W. Wilson Company

Wilson Catalog Card for a book of individual biography, suggesting only one classification number.

Mays, Willie Howard
   Born to play ball, by Willie Mays, as told to Charles Einstein. Putnam 1955
168p illus

The Negro player with the N. Y. Giants who has a natural ability to play ball "recapitulates some of the high points of his Major League career. . . Just a few spot souvenirs of an Alabama childhood and a ball-playing father and grandfather precede what is largely a chronology of the 1951 and 1954 seasons." Kirkus

1 Baseball I Einstein, Charles II Title   92 or 796.357

4-8-55   (W) The H. W. Wilson Company

Wilson Catalog Card for a book of individual biography, suggesting two possible classification numbers.

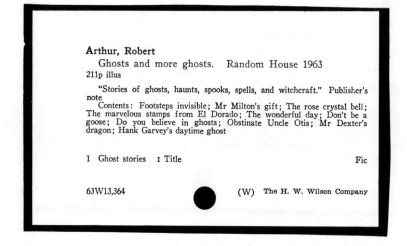

Arthur, Robert
    Ghosts and more ghosts.   Random House 1963
211p illus

   "Stories of ghosts, haunts, spooks, spells, and witchcraft." Publisher's
note
      Contents: Footsteps invisible; Mr Milton's gift; The rose crystal bell;
The marvelous stamps from El Dorado; The wonderful day; Don't be a
goose; Do you believe in ghosts; Obstinate Uncle Otis; Mr Dexter's
dragon; Hank Garvey's daytime ghost

   1   Ghost stories   ɪ Title   Fic

   63W13,364   ●   (W) The H. W. Wilson Company

Wilson Catalog Card for a book of fiction.

that these books which deal with one person's life all be
classified with one number for the ease of the user of the
collection. He will then look in one place in the library for
all books which present biographies.

It may be that your library will use 921 or 92 (a short
form of the number 921) for these individual biographies.
Or it may be that some other special coding such as the use
of the letter "B" (for *biography*) is used. But if the materials of this type are together, the user will probably be less
mystified than if the material is placed elsewhere.

Books about several people, collective biographies, will
be placed in the 920 classification group and will be, in all
probability, housed near the books of individual biographies. This is most practical in a small library.

A third kind of special case pertains to books of fiction—
those books which we usually call "story books". These are
books whose events never really happened, although similar
incidents might have occurred in real life. The people in

these books never really lived even though, in the book, they seem to be true to life to such a degree that they might have lived. When working with books of fiction, it is well to examine the title and the description of the book found on the dust jacket. Fiction may be identified by the subtitle of the book or by such expressions in the description as "a novel of . . .", or "a story of . . .", or "a narrative . . .". When you find such words as these, you are on fairly safe ground to consider the book one of fiction.

Printed catalog cards use the coding "Fic" in the lower right hand corner to identify these books. Generally, libraries will select from several ways of handling such books the one way most suitable. Fiction may be classified under the literature number—in the 800 group, depending upon the language of the book. Or fiction may be *unclassified*, using only the initial letter of the author's last name (or combinations of the letters) but no numbers. Or the short form of the work "fiction"—Fic—may be used in combination with the author initial. Again, if the collection has been in existence for some time, it is advisable to follow what has been established. If a decision is to be made, the simplest form—that of using only the author initials—is both suitable and usable.

B. When there are no printed catalog cards available.

When catalog cards prepared by professional librarians are not available, it becomes necessary to do the classification of books by using such tools and such techniques as are available. The following sequence may be helpful if you are depending almost entirely upon yourself and the books which we have referred to from time to time. There are three books so important to have that it is almost impossible to do without them: the *Children's Catalog*, the A.L.A. *Basic List* for elementary schools, and the *Dewey Decimal Classification Guide*.

1. Check the *Children's Catalog* and the A.L.A. *Basic List* to see if the title is included in the alphabetic list.

2. If it is included, a note of the classification number should be made on the work card. Then turn to the numbered section covering the books in this classification and find the page where the section begins.
Look through the titles listed to find the entry for this title. Read the entry.
Compare the entry with other entries in the section and if the title seems to fit into the pattern of content of the books included, use the number for this group.

3. If the title is not included in the alphabetic list, examine the book carefully to see what it is about. Check both the *Children's Catalog* and the A.L.A. *Basic List* to see if the subject you decided upon is included in this list. If it is, note the number on the work card and turn to the numbered section in the *Children's Catalog* which lists the books which have been given this classification number. Read through the descriptive notes on books which are included here to determine if they are really similar to the book you are working on. If so, use the number. If the descriptions are not about which are similar in content, try another subject and repeat this process.

4. If necessary, because of the lack of information found in the books mentioned above, for these titles, turn to the *Dewey Decimal Classification Guide*. Re-examine the book and try to see if you find an appropriate subject listing for this book in the alphabetic section of the book. Consult the numerical table, following the selection of a number, to try to decide if this number, or any other, includes the specific subject of this book.

5. It may be necessary, for your own information, to use a dictionary to help define the subject. This may prove to be most helpful in those areas where your own knowledge is a bit sketchy. In science, particularly, the average person is not, usually, as well informed as this particular job may require. The dictionary will, frequently, assist in clarifying the problem of selecting an appropriate subject name.

6. Again, use the classified section, going through the specific headings for comparison with the subject of the book. Select the one which seems most appropriate because it describes the subject area of the book best.

7. Turn back to the *Children's Catalog* and the A.L.A. *Basic List* and find the correct numbered section covering your selection. Again, compare the books listed with the one you are trying to classify, to see how similar the content is.

8. Repeat this process as it is necessary to until you find a number which seems appropriate for the book and which fits into the classification of other similar books in one of the references.

9. Assign this number to the book. Enter it on the work card in the appropriate place for use later on.

Generally, remember that when there are no available printed cards, the procedure becomes one in which you are the decision-making person. You will need to check all possible sources of information about the subject of the book. They may lead you to the fact that the best source is, as it should be, the book, itself. But few librarians can take time to read all the books which they classify. They must learn, as you are learning, to use short cuts and to put the knowledge of others to work for them. They may have more extensive reference materials, and they may have specialists to turn to, but, basically, they will be repeating the same processes as you are in greater depth and with a wider scope. They, too, will:

1. Check the book's cover, the preface, the introduction, the table of contents for clues to the contents of the book.
2. Compare what this reveals with other existing books, either directly (book with book) or indirectly (by using the descriptions of the books found in the references).
3. Compare the given classifications of these titles with the classification numbers in the *Dewey Decimal Classification Guide.*
4. Consult any available authorities (such as already established catalog cards, new printed cards, other books, other libraries, people who are specialists).
5. Select the most appropriate number and assign it.

Classification and Processing

Having decided upon the classification number, we now may proceed to apply it to the processing of the book. It may be that in receiving the books, the order cards have been taken from the file to become work cards. If not, do so now. Begin by finding the order card in the file of cards you set up when you were preparing to order the printed catalog cards. This is now, you will recall, an alphabetic list—alphabetic by author and, within the same author's group, by title. Remove this card from the file. Be sure that the card has on it this information: author, title, publisher, date of publication (or copyright), place of publication, cost, number of pages, illustrator and illustrations note, any necessary series note, the classification number and the accession number.

The card will now look like this:

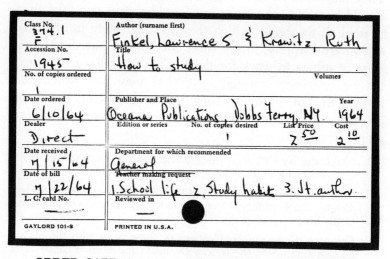

ORDER CARD, in use as work card **after receipt of book.**

Below the classification number write the first initial of the author's last name unless the book is an individual biography which is being classified in the 900 section, using 921 or 92 or B. If the book is an individual biography, use the first initial of the last name of the subject of the book—the person about whom the book is written.

Examples:

1. Author: Webster, Noah
   Title: Dictionary of the English language
   Classification number and author initial: 423
                                                            W

2. Author: Robert Frost
   Title: Poems
   Classification number and author initial: 811
                                                            F

3. Author: John Smith
   Title: Authors I have known
   Classification number and author initial: 920
                                                     S

4. Author: Susan Adams
   Title: George Washington as a boy
   Classification number and author initial: 92
                                                     W

5. Author: Crowler Peters
   Title: The leader of the Revolution—Washington
   Classification number and author initial: 92
                                                     W

6. Author: Mary Jane Doe
   Title: Washington as a colonial farmer
   Classification number and author initial: 92
                                                     W

This combination of the classification number and the initial letter of the author's last name (or, for individual biography, the initial letter of the subject of the book) is termed the *call number* of the book. This term refers to the use of these numbers in that we use them when we "call for" a book to be brought to us from the library shelves.

Write this call number in the following places in the book:

1. on the upper left-hand corner of the book pocket.
2. on the upper left-hand corner of the lining paper at the back of the book.
3. on the book card, in the upper left-hand corner.
   Note: remember that when the end papers (lining papers) are decorated, the pocket, the date due slip, and the markings are moved to the inside of the lining papers.

This call number should be added in two more places. It should be written in pencil on the back of the title page. It should be added to the spine of the book. For this last purpose, use the guide which was prepared earlier, letter the spine using the ink and method of your choice. Then, when the lettering is dry, spray with prepared spray or cover lightly with a clear and thin coat of shellac. Let this dry completely before handling the book.

Remember, too, that if you are using plastic covers, the call number will be typed on the gummed label which will be affixed to the plastic cover.

This step completes the physical processing of the book.

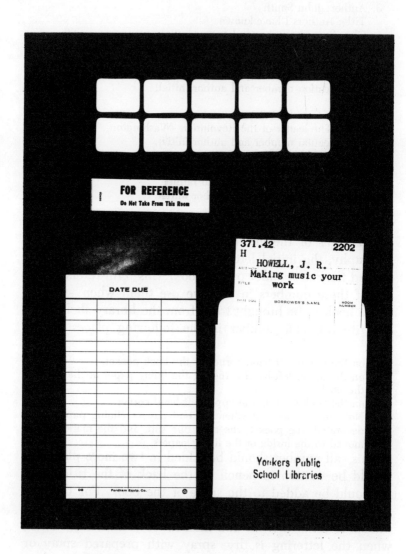

Supplies for the physical processing of the book.

8

Cataloging Books

The Purpose of Cataloging Books

One of the ways of making a library useful to its readers is to have a simple way of telling people what is in the library. We have learned that the process of classification of the books helps to give certain kinds of information about the collection to the users. There is a second process which we apply to all materials which extends the work begun by classifying them.

This procedure is cataloging the book. This process attempts to select a variety of topics or subject headings which describe the contents of the book accurately. After the selection is made, these selections must be presented to the reader or made available to him in such a way that he may readily see not only the nature of one book, but also the relationship which exists between this book and all other materials in the library.

We try to extend this service, too, by "giving directions" to the reader if he needs them. We do this through the developing of an index to all the materials of the collection in much the same way that a book's index provides the reader with a key to the book. The cataloging process makes it possible to have such a key for the entire library collection. This index is usually made available to the user in the form

of a file of cards. The cards contain the information about
the collection and are compact enough to be used easily.
And by using cards, the index remains flexible, changing
as the book collection becomes larger or smaller, incorpor-
ating with a minimum of effort new information about the
new books.

Major Problems in Cataloging

In cataloging a book there are, basically, four questions
to be answered.

1. Who wrote the book and what is the correct form of the author's
   name?
2. What subjects does the book cover and are the sub-topics included sufficiently important to require calling attention to them?
3. What are the related subjects that might be referred to or used
   in trying to discover the contents of this book? How do we relate
   these to the main subjects of the book?
4. What are the other ways in which the book can be described?

Any one of these questions can be answered in volumes.
And there are about as many ways of handling each problem as there are librarians doing the job of cataloging. For
our purposes, however, we will try to establish some simple
ways of making the cataloging process understandable, functional, and possible.

The author's name: It is still customary to use the real
name of the authors of books rather than made-up names
or names-which have been changed. However, there is one
group of librarians, and it is an expanding group, which
holds that if the made-up name, the pseudonym, is better
known than the real one, the name which is best known
should be used. The reason for this thinking is a straight-
forward and utilitarian one. This is the name that the library's users know. For a small library, this is quite acceptable if it seems most practical to do so. If, however, it is expected that the library will grow or be a part of a library
system, it may be better to follow the established pattern
for the sake of avoiding confusion and change later on.

Regardless of which system is finally selected, it will be necessary to establish a uniformity for each author's name so that his name will always be spelled in the same manner; the same use of given names or initials will be found when reference is made to his writings; there will be referral from the various forms which are known to the authoritative form; if pseudonyms are used, there will be referral from this form to the authoritative form.

One example of a name form which has many variations is that of William Shakespeare. Known forms used in the materials of Shakespeare's life use many different spellings. There is SHAKESPERE; SHAKSPERE; SHAKSPER. The generally accepted form is the first example above—Shakespeare.

One author who is known as much by his pseudonym as by his real name is Samuel Clemens or Mark Twain. Many people probably never think of this author as being Mr. Clemens. However Clemens is his real name and it is important that this be known. Many libraries would make entries under both names; many more would refer from the pseudonym to the real name; some fewer ones would use the pseudonym because it is so generally known.

The name which is going to be used must be used uniformly from the time of its selection until all materials by this individual are withdrawn from the library. To establish the correct name, use one of the following as your authority and your guide: the *Children's Catalog*; A.L.A. *Basic List;* any standard encyclopedia (for well-established writers), biographical lists in standard dictionaries, other authoritative reference books or documents.

Subjects and sub-topics: This is one of the jobs which will call for thought and serious reflection and an inquiring mind to seek out the information necessary. To answer the question, "What is this book about?" you will need to learn what is in the book. The title, the table of contents, the book itself may all be sources of information. In addition, the classification number which has been assigned to the book was selected on the basis of the book's subject. That information, the classification number, can be looked up in both the *Children's Catalog* and in the A.L.A. *Basic List* to see what the general subject covered by the number includes. This is a good time, too, to make use of the *Dewey Decimal Classfication Guide*, for it, too, lists the numbers with their assigned subjects.

It is also helpful for the librarian to begin to think of all the possible ways in which a user of the library would think about this book if he would want to use it. What are the words he would use to describe it? These suggested descriptive words should be looked up in the three books mentioned above, in the alphabetic lists, to see if they are included or if they refer you to some other subject.

It is customary to think first of the general subject of the book, as defined in the classification system, and then to see how this general subject can be broken down into subdivisions. There are several commonly accepted types of subdivisions used in most libraries. Perhaps the best known of these is the type which represents a part of the larger whole subject. A book about folk songs, for example, is a book about a part of the general subject of music. Another of the types of subdivisions used frequently is the geographical section covered by the book. A third type involves the time period covered by the book. This has great use in the general field of history or in any portion of a subject where the time period is significant. The fourth common method of subdivision is by literary form. Some material about a subject may be in story form, as in the example of a story about animals. Or it may be in the form of poetry or an essay or a bibliography about the subject. There are other kinds of subdivisions, but these four are widely used and easily identified.

The last section in this chapter will give instructions for using the various resources in finding and selecting these subdivision headings and the general headings. The step-by-step sequence given there will extend this general discussion of the kinds of divisions to look for.

Related subjects: For small libraries, it is a good general practice to use main subjects only for cataloging purposes. As a library's collection grows, however, it may be necessary for the catalog to grow also so that it will take the place of the personal examination of the books by the user. When there are few books to check, there is less need of detailed descriptions of the books. When there are many books, the detailed descriptions will be time-savers for the reader.

Generally, it will be necessary to choose from these related subjects those which are most helpful and to refer from those which are not used to the ones which are being used. This sequence is described in the following chapter.

Other kinds of listings: There are many kinds of possible listings for the library's materials, and some books will require extensive listings while others can be relatively simple. The examples given here may help you make decisions about the particular books you are working with.

1. Joint authors. If the book has more than one author, the names of these authors, up to about three, should be used as additional entries for the book. If a great many famous people have acted jointly as authors, it may be necessary to include all of them.

2. Illustrator's names should be used as entries.

3. Parts of the book may need to be mentioned. These are called "analytics" and refer just to a portion of the book. Examples might include books of short stories, books about several people, books about several related subjects. In the case of the short stories, several or all of these stories might be well-known by name. In such case they will require special listing. When a collected biography includes several famous people, each person may require special

mention. And special parts of books will need special mention.

A practical example of this last type is a book about careers within a certain area, such as science careers. Such a book might have one section on careers in biology. Another section of the book might deal with careers in the area of atomic energy developments. And a third section might pertain to careers in the study of astronomy. Each of these sections need to be called to the attention of the library user.

4. Listings may need to be made for subjects which are not used, giving the library patron directions in where he should look to find what he wants. An example of this might be as follows:

ATOMIC POWER   (this heading is not used

    see   (turn to

ATOMIC ENERGY   (this heading which is used.

5. For some materials in special format or of special types, this type of material rather than its content is the subject heading which should be used. One example of the use of the form is in regard to encyclopedias. For all sets of encyclopedias and for one-volume encyclopedias the heading ENCYCYOPEDIAS should be used. It would be impossible to define all the subjects included in the content of an encyclopedia since so many different subjects and different facets of one subject are presented. Consequently, this word, which describes both a special type and a special format is used.

For encyclopedias dealing with only one general subject, both the general term and the specific subject area would be mentioned. An example of this might be: ENCYCLOPEDIAS—SCIENCE.

Using the Printed Catalog Cards

If you have printed catalog cards for the book, the cataloging for it has been done. Look at the Wilson Cards or the Library of Congress cards which have been made for this book. You will note that toward the bottom of the card there are several topics listed following either Roman numerals or Arabic numerals. These topics include the catalog headings. They have been selected by professionally trained librarians. Note the example below.

371.42 **Nourse, Alan E**
  N   So you want to be a nurse, by Alan E. Nourse with
       Eleanore Halliday. Harper 1961
       186p

     2868

     1 Nursing as a profession ı Halliday, Eleanore ıı Title   610.73

    61W10.864   ●   (W) The H. W. Wilson Company

Notice, also, that in this sample card the subject headings are printed on the top line and that the heading is in all capital letters. This is the form used for the subject cards both in printed form and in typed form. In the next chapter there will be a full explanation of this card as well as of other forms used for each kind of card.

Cataloging Without Printed Cards

When printed catalog cards are not available, other aids may be used to help determine what subject headings describe the book. Again we turn to the two basic references which serve the library so well—the *Children's Catalog* and the *Basic List* published by the American Library Association.

Turn to the classified section of each of these lists and look for an entry for one book which appears in both of them. We have, below, such a sample.

Entry taken from the
Children's Catalog
Tenth edition. 1961

Schwartz, Julius
Through the magnifying glass; little things that make a big difference; pictures by Jeanne Bendick. McGray 1954 142 p illus. (Whittlesey House publications) $2.75 (5-8)   500

1. Science 2. Scientific recreations

Analytics

Animals p81-102
Lenses p11-18
Plants p51-80

Entry taken from the
A.L.A. *Basic Book
Collection.* . . .
1956 ed.

SCHWARTZ, JULIUS. Through the Magnifying Glass; il. by Jeanne Bendick. Whittlesey, 1954. $2.50 (5-7) 500 Microscopes   (W)

Note that the suggested subject entries are not the same. The *Children's Catalog* suggests two subject headings—Science, and Scientific recreations—for this book. The A.L.A.

list suggests only one—Microscopes. Actually, in looking at the book and in considering how to make the cataloging cover as many different kinds of possibilities as the users of the library might come up with, it may be the best decision to make entries for all three of these subject entries rather than to limit oneself to either model. Note, too, that the *Children's Catalog* entry contains three analytics—entries for a part of the book each of three additional subjects. And it may be desirable to have these included also. If that were the final decision, then, there would be six subject headings in all for the book—three regular subject headings and three analytics.

It might be well to explain that each of these entries was prepared by professionally trained librarians, but that the composition of the groups actually making the final decisions was different. This is not unusual. Whenever there is a difference in two librarians' interpretations of books, there is, merely, evidence that not everyone thinks in the same way. Decisions do have to be made and decisions may differ without being "wrong". The final and ultimate test of the decision which is made comes from the users of the collection. If they can find their ways about the library's materials easily and with satisfactory results, the library is functional no matter what the decision was.

When we find, in this case, that reliable references are not identical in their interpretations, it should not disturb us. Rather, it should encourage the examination, more closely, of the entries which are suggested and should assist in making the catalog more useful.

When there are no printed cards and when there is no entry for the book in any of the basic lists, the problems of cataloging the book rests completely on the librarian. This is, actually, a job for the professional librarian, but when there is no professionally trained person to do the work, it is better to have it completed by someone who will try to do an acceptable job even though it will not be expert than it is to have nothing done. There are a few procedures and a few devices which can be of very practical help in doing this work. In addition to the list given in the first chapter, these titles may also be very helpful:

Akers, Susan Grey. *Simple library cataloging.* Chicago, American Library Association, 1954. Fourth edition. $5.00.

Johnson, Margaret Fullerton; and Cook, Dorothy E. *Manual of cataloging and classification for small school and public libraries.* New York, H. W. Wilson, 1950. Fourth edition.

Plan, also, to refer to the book by Rue on subject headings and to the Dewey classification manual, both mentioned on page 9.

Here is a practical sequence of steps to follow:

1. If the book is classified turn to the basic lists and find this classified section. See if the title is listed. If it is, the work of cataloging will be included in the entry, as you have seen. If the title is not included, compare the book with similar materials which are listed. Note especially the subject headings used for books in the same category. Compare the table of contents of the book with the subject headings. If they seem to be similar, check the section in the book which seem particularly to fit, to verify your judgment. When it is confirmed, write the subject headings which are appropriate for the book on the work card (previously the order card). This should be in the pocket of the book. Write as many of the headings as are necessary or desirable.

   If there is not space for all this information on the face of the card, turn it over and make the entries there. When this is done, it will be helpful to write the word "over" on the face of the card as a direction to whoever will be doing the typing.

2. Check the headings selected with the list in the book by Rue, *Subject Headings for Children's Materials.* If these headings are listed there, use them. If not, try to think of other terms which carry the same meaning and go through this sequence with the new subjects.

3. Using the *Abridged Dewey Decimal Classification Guide,* turn to the alphabetic list to see if the selected subjects are included. If so, they may be used.

4. Check also the alphabetic section of the two basic lists to see if the selected subjects are used.

5. If the subjects you are thinking of using are found in at least two of these resource materials, it is important to use that subject as an entry for the book.

Each of these subject headings and "added entries" which you will be developing will require that a catalog card be typed using this heading on the first line. Thus, one book may have as many as thirty or forty cards and another may have only three.

All of these cards will have to be properly typed, following a standard form. Using such a form will simplify the work of the typist and will also make it possible for the user of the library to follow what has been done more easily. Chapter IX gives the necessary instructions for typing catalog cards of all kinds.

When the cards have been typed, they are put into a card file, called the card catalog, because it is an index or catalog in card form. This extensive set of cards then becomes a complete index to the entire book collection and provides a guide to the user in his search for information. Chapter IX treats, also, of the method used in filing the catalog cards.

9

The Card Catalog

The Function of the Card Catalog

The card catalog is the over-all index to the entire collection of the library. It may be compared to the index of a book. The index tells two major things—it tells what is in the book and it tells on what page you will find each item mentioned in the index. The card catalog should provide the same kind of information about the materials of the library. It should list what there is in the library and it should reveal how these materials are located.

The way in which the card catalog is developed will determine how well it will be able to fulfill these two purposes. If the cataloging process is a complete one, the card catalog will be a good index to the collection. If the cataloging is done in a hap-hazard fashion, it will provide hap-hazard information about the collection.

In addition, it is extremely important to develop and to use a method of putting down the information about the materials—a pattern of recording this information—so that it is simple for the user of the library to discover what he needs to know. It is for this reason, that the methods described in this chapter have been developed. These forms will make the catalog both simple and practical for it is uncomplicated.

Developing Catalog Cards

The Unit System: By now, you have noted that there are certain kinds of information about a book which identify it. You have made use of this information in preparing to order the book, in accessioning it, in cataloging it. Now you will make use of much of this same information in developing the card catalog.

The card catalog is made up of many individual cards, each referring to a particular book or to a particular subject or author in the collection. Ordinarily each book needs to have several cards—an author card, a title card, and as many subject cards as are necessary to describe the book. If each of these cards was made out in whatever way that we felt like using at the particular time, it might prove to be simple enough for us to use the catalog, but it would be extremely awkward for anyone else to attempt to use it. So we develop and use a standardized form, make adaptations of it for various purposes, and relate each kind to the other kinds.

Let us examine two sets of printed cards, prepared by the H. W. Wilson Company, for two different books. The first set of cards (overlapped for the sake of convenience) has printed classification numbers and printed catalog headings (subject headings and other added entries) for the book. The second set has neither the numbers nor the headings, but has only the basic descriptive information about the book included.

Look closely at the first set of sample cards. Compare the information on each card with what is on each of the other cards and you will discover two very important facts: one card is a shorter form than all of the other cards; and all the other cards are alike except for the first line. The card with the short form will become the shelf list card, and this kind of card and its uses will be discussed in the next chapter. All the other cards, regardless of the differences in headings, will become a part of the card catalog.

HOW TO ORGANIZE A CHILDREN'S LIBRARY

Frick, Bertha Margaret, 1894-   ed.
025.33 Sears list of subject headings; with suggestions for the be-

SUBJECT HEADINGS

025.33 **Sears** list of subject headings; with suggestions for the be-
ginner in subject heading work. 8th ed. by Bertha Margaret Frick.   Wilson, H.W. 1959
610p

025.33   **Sears** list of subject headings; with suggestions for the be-
ginner in subject heading work. 8th ed. by Bertha Mar-
garet Frick.   Wilson, H.W. 1959
610p

First published 1923 as List of subject headings for small libraries,
by Minnie Earl Sears. The 1959 edition has been thoroughly revised and
brought up-to-date. This list follows the Library of Congress headings,
abridged to meet the needs of the smaller libraries. The classification
numbers have been assigned by the Decimal Classification Editorial Office
from the (8th) Abridged Dewey Decimal classifications

1 Subject headings   1 Frick, Bertha Margaret, 1894-   ed.
025.33

59W5,529   ●   (W) The H. W. Wilson Company

025.33   **Sears** list of subject headings; with suggestions for the be-
ginner in subject heading work. 8th ed. by Bertha Margaret Frick.   Wilson, H.W. 1959
610p

1 Subject headings 1 Frick, Bertha Margaret, 1894-   ed.   025.33

59W5,529   ●   (W) The H. W. Wilson Company

Let us examine each kind of card, using the shelf list card, the short form, as our point of departure. The short form, the shelf list card, has the classification number in the upper left-hand corner of the card. To the right of this number is the author's name, with the last name appearing first and with the given name (and initial or middle name) coming after the surname. On the second line of this card we find the title of the book, the place where the book was published, the publisher, and the date of publication or copyright. This second part seems to be in paragraph form and continues from one line to the next as necessary. This paragraph may also contain a note concerning the edition of the book or a note mentioning people other than the author who have been responsible for it—usually an editor, a joint author, or an illustrator. Following this information there seems to be a small and irregular paragraph which describes the book physically, giving its paging, information about its illustrations, and any information about additional volumes or parts of a series. At the very bottom of the card, to the extreme right, in small print, you will find the Dewey Decimal Classification number. If there are several possible numbers from which to choose, there may be several numbers given in this place.

If we turn now to the other cards, looking at them closely, we may notice that each of them contains this same information, plus something else. Each of the cards, except one, has a different first line. This first line identifies the kind of catalog card it is and is called the "entry". When the first line is a subject heading, the card is a "subject card". When the first line is the author's name, the card is an "author card". When the first line is the name of a second author who helped write the book, the card is a "joint author card". When the first line is the name of the person who provided the pictures for the book, the card is an "illustrator's card". We give to the first line the term "entry", so that we may call these first lines "subject entry", "author entry", "joint author entry", etc. because it is under these words that the card is "entered" in the catalog.

Notice, also, that with all the different first lines for the cards for this one book, there are several which have the first line printed in all capital letters. The use of capital letters for the entire heading marks the card as a "subject entry". Subject headings are always printed in all capital letters.

Following these first lines which are different, notice that the author's name comes on the next line. This is typical of all cards.

The paragraph which starts with the title of the book is called the "imprint". It contains, usually, the information found on the title page of the book, and this information is given in almost the same form as it appears on the title page. It includes, in most cases, the title, joint authors and editors, illustrators, editions notes, place of publication, publisher, and date (the year) of the publication of the book.

The next section of the cards is like the small paragraph of the shelf list card, too. This "almost paragraph" in smaller type contains the physical description of the book—paging, illustrations note, etc. This physical description is called the "collation".

Then follows, on all except the shelf list card, a description of the contents of the book. This may be a quotation from some authority and when it has not been prepared by the staff of the H. W. Wilson Company, it is in quotation marks and the authority is quoted.

At the lower part of the card appear the various entries for the book. Compare the printed names of the entries from this part of the card with the first lines appearing on the cards for the book. Note that for every item listed at the bottom of the card there is a card with this item on the first line. This list of entries on the bottom of the cards is called the "tracing". The name explains its use. It is used to trace the cards in the catalog for this particular book. We will refer again to the tracing in Chapter ten, when we discuss the shelf list, and in chapter eleven, when we discuss the problems of maintaining the collection.

Immediately below is the second set of sample cards. This set does not have all the entries printed at the top and it does not have the classification numbers printed in the upper left-hand corner. All of the cards in this set, with the exception of the shelf list card, the short form, are alike. The shelf list card for this set is like the shelf list card for

Slobodkin, Louis   illus.
Unnerstad, Edith
    Pysen; illus. by Louis Slobodkin.   Macmillan 1955

SWEDEN—FICTION
Unnerstad, Edith
    Pysen; illus. by Louis Slobodkin.   Macmillan 1955

Pysen
Unnerstad, Edith
    Pysen; illus. by Louis Slobodkin.   Macmillan 1955
    172p illus

Unnerstad, Edith
    Pysen; illus. by Louis Slobodkin.   Macmillan 1955
    172p illus

        Translated from the Swedish by Inger Boye
        Humorous episodes and adventures in the life of curious five-year-old
    Pysen Larsson of the Swedish Larssons in "The saucepan journey"

    1 Sweden—Fiction   ɪ Slobodkin, Louis   illus.   ɪɪ Title
                                                                  jFic

    3-11-55   ●   (W)   The H. W. Wilson Company

Catalog Cards without printed classification numbers.

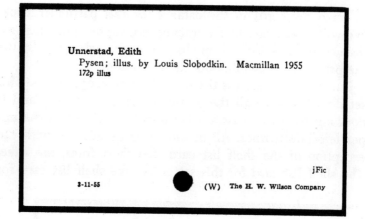

Shelf List card for the set above.

the first set of sample cards except for the omission of the classification number. And it is different from the other cards in this set only in not having the summary of the book and in not having the tracing.

You will note, however, that the catalog cards do have the book summary and, at the bottom, do have the tracing and the Dewey classification number.

To summarize, the H. W. Wilson Company prints sets of cards both with classification numbers and subject headings and without classification numbers or subject headings. All sets of cards for any book will have the necessary cards included—author, title, and as many subject cards as are necessary. There will be a shelf list card for every book. All of the cards in the set will have the same information: author, imprint, collation, classification number. In addition, the catalog cards will have a descriptive note about the book and the tracing for the book.

The use of this basic information on all the cards for a book is called the "unit system". If this system is used throughout the card catalog and the shelf list of a library, it is simple for the patrons of the library to become acquainted with it and to learn how to use the information on the cards. The use of a standard form is always less complicated for the library patron than is the use of unrelated forms.

Completing the Printed Catalog Cards: When the library is using printed catalog cards, it is a fairly simple job to complete them. The sequence which follows will be of assistance in setting up an orderly procedure which can serve as a guide to prevent errors.

1. Complete the call number of the book (the classification number and the author initial) on every card in the set.

   a. It will be necessary to check the classification number printed on the card to be certain that this number is the one to be used. You will recall that in discussing books on different vocations, for example, it was suggested that all books dealing with any vocations be classified as 371.42 rather than scattering them throughout the collection. And you will recall that some books may, correctly, be placed in several categories, depending upon the selection of one interpretation rather than another. If it is necessary to select or to change printed numbers, make the necessary correction, erasing any numbers to be changed, and typing the selected number in the proper place.

   b. Add the initial of author's last name, just below the classification number, in the upper left-hand corner, except for books of individual biography. These titles will use the initial of the last name of the SUBJECT of the book instead of the author or the book.

   c. For books of fiction, small libraries will probably prefer to omit using any classification number and to use only the initial letter of the author's last name as the complete call number.

2. Subject headings will need to be checked against those given at the bottom of the card to be sure that the set is complete. If the printed cards being used do not have the subject headings printed at the top, these headings will have to be added.

   a. One subject heading only on any one card.

   b. The subject heading is added to the card one line above the author's name.

   c. Begin the subject heading 3 typing spaces to the right of the first letter of the author's name as it is entered on the card.

   d. Type the subject heading completely in capital letters.

   e. Follow exactly the wording and any punctuation or abbreviations as they are given on the lower part of the card.

3. A title card must be available for every book.

   a. The title is placed one line above the author's name, three spaces to the right of the first letter of the author's name as it appears on the card.

   b. Use the title as it appears on the printed card.

   c. Capitalize only the first letter of the first word of the title unless a proper name is a part of the title. Proper names are capitalized within the title.

   d. Put a period after the last letter of the title.

4. Additional cards needed for joint authors, editors, illustrators, etc., may be developed as below.

   a. Begin typing the name one line above the author's name on the card and 3 spaces to the right of the first letter of the author's name.

   b. Use the last name of the individual first, and use a capital letter for the beginning of each name.

   c. Follow the surname with a comma, add the given name (or initials if the given name is unknown) and then use another comma.

   d. Add the proper abbreviation to indicate this person's relationship to the book and place a period after it. Select the proper designation from this list. If the individual is a:

joint author,	use	jt. auth.
illustrator,	use	illus.
editor,	use	ed.
compiler,	use	comp.

Note the example in the second set of cards opposite page 109.

   e. Note: If the person's name is to be used as the subject of the book, follow the instructions given in item #2.

5. All shelf list cards will require two additions, and some may require an additional item.

   a. Complete the call number for the book, typing it in the upper left-hand corner. This may require adding the classification number plus the author initial or it may require changing the number and adding the initial, or it may require only adding the initial.

   b. Add to the card, 3 lines below the collation (physical description of the book) and to the right of the first letter of the author's name, the accession number of the book. (See examples in Chapter Ten).

   c. If this book is one of several copies, add the accession numbers of all copies of the book and mark each accession number with the proper copy number. Use this form:

    621, c.1
    780, c.2
    781, c.3

d. If this book is one volume of a set, all with the same name, add all accession numbers for all volumes, and mark each accession number with the correct volume number, following this form:

    247, v.1   249, v.3   251, v.5
    248, v.2   250, v.4

Make colums as far as space will allow to try to get all volumes and their accession numbers on the one card.

Typing Unprinted Catalog Cards: If there is no money to buy the printed catalog cards, and, in addition, for those books which do not have printed catalog cards available, it will be necessary to develop the information for the cards for each book and to type the cards. It is practical to use the work cards for this purpose, recording the information there until it is possible to type the entire set of cards for the book. Some information about the book is already on the work cards. If it should be necessary to change any part of this information, draw a red line through the original entry and add the correct information. It will also be necessary to use the book, itself, for developing the information which will be used for the catalog and shelf list cards.

1. The author's name: Use the title page of the book as the authority for the author's name. Be sure that the name on the work card is correct. If the title page gives only initials, leave space to add the full name when some other authority indicates the full correct name.

2. The title: Examine the title page to determine the correct title of the book. This, too, should be compared with the title as it appears on the work card and, if the work card is wrong, correction should be made.

3. Other imprint information: Check also, and correct as necessary: the place of publication, the publisher; the date of publication or copyright. If the date does not appear on the title page, it

may appear on the back of the page. If this is the case, write
the information on the work card and put brackets [ ] around it.
For example, if the title page has no date of printing and no
copyright date on it, but the back of the title page includes the
words: "copyright 1964," this information would be written
[c1964]. Sometimes the letter *c* is used instead of the word
"copyright" on the back of the title page.

4. Make any necessary additions to cover joint authors, illustrators,
editors, etc.

5. The collation will require paging and illustrations notes, plus
series entries. For children's libraries it is quite suitable to use
the short form for the collation, using only the paging for the
main section of the book. Some books have extensive introduc-
tions with separate paging, and some have indexes and various
sections at the back with separate paging, also. For a small
library this information is not as necessary as it is for a very
scholarly library. Look at the last numbered page in the book's
major section. Write that number on the work card, on the bottom line, and follow the number by the letter "p" for pages.
Your notation will look like this: 310 p.

6. Next examine the illustrations and make a note of the particular
type they represent, using the appropriate abbreviations from
the list:

illus.   general types of illustrations
pl.   used for colored reproductions
phot.   when illustrations are photographs
maps   when there are several important maps

If the end papers are highly decorative, particularly if this deco-
ration gives additional information to the content of the book, it
may be important to mention that, using this form for such
notation: (end maps). Use parentheses.

7. If the book is one of several volumes, do not use a paging note.
Instead, use the number of volumes in the set. For example, the
cards for a set of encyclopedias would not include paging for
each volume or for the set. Instead, the total number of volumes
in the set would be indicated in this manner: 21v.

8. Be sure that the work card includes the call number (developed
and described in chapter seven) and the subject headings to be
used (developed in chapter eight). The subject headings will be
used not only to type the subject cards, but to record the tracing
information for the book.

Typing the Cards: We are now ready to take the information from the work cards and put it into the correct form on the cards for the catalog and the shelf list. The method presented here will use the unit systems which was discussed earlier, and which was analyzed using the printed examples.

For the catalogs it is customary to use a standard sized card, about 3″ x 5″, punched near the lower edge so as to receive a metal rod from the filing cabinet where the cards will be housed. These cards may be purchased from any of the standard supply houses for libraries or from a stationer. There are many different weights of cards, at different prices. It is desirable to use a card of no less than medium weight and of good quality so that it will take the handling which will be given it. Completely blank cards may be used, or the cards selected may have printed guide lines. Note that in the sample, there are both horizontal and vertical guides.

In giving the following instructions, reference will be made to "first indention" and "second indention" and "third indention". If you are using ruled cards, the first verticle line will represent the first indention. A second vertical line (from the left) will represent the second indention, and so on.

If the cards are blank, the following spacings and terms to describe them will be used:

first indention: 11 spaces from the left edge of the card.
second indention: 13 spaces from the left of the card.
third indention: 15 spaces from the left edge of the card.

Begin by developing, either on the work card, or in your mind, or directly on the card to be typed, the "unit". Here is an example:

This information will be used on every card developed for this book. The form above may actually become the author card. And the same information constitutes the "unit".

371.3   Finkel, Lawrence S
F   How to study, by Lawrence S. Finkel and Ruth
          Krawitz: illus. by Duane Unkefer. Dobbs Ferry, N.Y.,
          Oceana, 1964.
             64 p. illus.

Notice one difference between the author card developed above and the printed examples. We have not added anything below the unit. There is no summary of the book; there is no classification number at the bottom; there is no tracing on the card. We save time and space by eliminating the summary; the classification number appears at the top of the card; the tracing will be placed on the shelf list card. The next chapter will explain this in detail.

For a book which has no author, we would use the following as the unit.

R
031   The World book encyclopedia. Chicago, Ill., Field
W   Enterprises, 1964.
             20v. illus. maps.

Note that we have followed the spacing on the first line, using the title as if it were the author, but that in the rest of the entry we have spaced the items as if they were appearing as part of the imprint. The collation is the same for this as it would be if there were an author.

Let us use our first example again, putting it into the correct form for a title card.

```
              Unkefer, Duane, illus.                    Card for
    371.4   Finkel, Lawrence S.                          Illustra-
    F              How to study, by Lawrence S. Finkel    tor of
              and Ruth Krawitz; illus. by Duane Unkefer.  the book
              Dobbs Ferry, N.Y., Oceana, 1964.
                63p. illus.
```

Notice that the "unit" information is used in the exact form developed for the author card, and that there is only one addition to the unit—the placing of the title at the top of the card, one typing line above the beginning of the "unit". Notice, also, that the title begins at the second indention in this line just as it begins at the second indention within the "unit".

The next kind of card which must be developed for the book is the subject card. Actually, a book may have several subject cards. The form for each will be the same, but the first line of each will be different. Note the two examples below. They are for the same book, and there are two different subject headings because it was decided (chapter eight) that the library user might look for material on this subject under either heading.

Example
No. 1 of
Subject
Card

          STUDY HABITS
371.4   Finkel, Lawrence S
F   How to study, by Lawrence S. Kinkel
          and Ruth Krawitz; illus. By Duane Unkefer.
          Dobbs Ferry, N.Y., Oceana, 1964.
          63p. illus.

Example
No. 2 of
Subject
Card

          SCHOOL LIFE
371.4   Finkel, Lawrence S
F   How to study, by Lawrence S. Kinkel
          and Ruth Krawitz; illus. by Duane Unkefer.
          Dobbs Ferry, N.Y., Oceana, 1964.
          63p. illus.

It is most important to remember that all subject headings are typed in all capital letters. This procedure assists both the user of the library and the librarian to identify easily what a book is about. Occasionally there are books with titles which are misleading, or the author of many books may be, himself, the subject of a book. In cases such as this, the capital letters on the card will point out that the wording on this first line represents the subject of the book and nothing else.

These three types of cards which have been illustrated so far represent the three major types of catalog cards which will need to be developed for each book. Remember that each book is different from other books in its form and in the way its content is presented. But there are also ways in which books are similar. Both of these characteristics are

brought out in the classification and cataloging processes—
how these particular books, in themselves, may be described
and how they fit into the rest of the collection.

Added Entries

In addition to the author and the title and the subject
cards, it is sometimes necessary or desirable to add to the
catalog other information about the book. If we remember
that the primary use of the card catalog is to help the boys
and girls find their way to the materials they wish or need,
some of the additional kinds of cards which will help describe the book become evident.

Books which have two authors need, for the most part, to
have the book listed under both authors. Sometimes the illustrator of the book is a very famous person and sometimes
the illustrations are so attractive that we want to call special
attention to them. In these cases, a card with the illustrator's name at the top is very helpful. Still another kind of
card which can be helpful to the user is the card which
lists the title of a series of books if there are several books
planned as a group with a group title, but also having individual titles. This kind of card would be called a series
card.

Most of these "added entries" make use of the unit of information which is the basis of the author, title, and subject
cards. Note, in the examples given below, how it appears.

Joint		Krawitz, Ruth, jt. auth.
Author	371.4	Finkel, Lawrence S
Card	F	How to study, by Lawrence S. Finkel
		and Ruth Krawitz; illus. by Duane Unkefer.
		Dobbs Ferry, N.Y., Oceana, 1964.
		63p. illus.

In the example of the joint author card the "unit" was used in full. In each case, the additional information included was added above the unit, beginning at the second indention. Such spacing sets off the information so that it is readily identified for what it is, yet it permits, too, that the basic structure of all of the catalog cards remains the same. This similarity helps make the card catalog easy to use.

The next kind of added entry which we mentioned was the card for what we call a series of books—a group of books with a general subject common to each and all of the books. But each book in the group presents a different facet or part of this general subject. Series of books frequently have a name to cover the entire group of books with each book of this series having its own name as well.

One of the well-known series of books for young people is a series called The Landmark Books, published by Random House. Each of the books in this series has an individual author and an individual title. They are alike in format, and all of them treat of some phase of the growth of the United States or the role of some one in contributing to the growth and development of the United States. To demonstrate how to approach this problem—recording information about the series through the catalog cards—we will use two titles from this series.

The first sample for this purpose is the book *The Erie Canal*, written by Samuel Hopkins Adams, illustrated by Leonard Vosburgh, published by Random House in 1953. That information would be available from the title page of the book. From examining the book we would learn that it had 182 pages and had illustrations and maps. The title page would also reveal that the book was one title in a series. This particular book, then, would need the following catalog cards: author, title, illustrator, subject(s), and series. Note how the information is presented on the following cards:

```
974.7   Adams, Samuel Hopkins                              Author Card
A           The Erie Canal; illus. by Leonard Vosburgh.   Note the de-
        N.Y., Random House, 1953.                          velopment of
            182p. illus. map. (Landmark Books)             the "unit."
```

The second card in the group is the title card and it follows the general directions for all title cards—use the basic unit with the addition of the title on the first line.

```
            The Erie Canal.                                Sample Title
974.7   Adams, Samuel Hopkins                              Card for a
A           The Erie Canal; illus. by Leonard Vosburgh.   book in a
        N.Y., Random House, 1953.                          series.
            182p. illus. map. (Landmark Books)
```

The subject card follows the same general pattern—use the basic unit with the addition of the subject heading on the first line, in all capital letters. It is interesting to note that for this book the subject heading is very similar to the title. The capitalization of the subject heading will, however, set the two apart in their meaning to the user.

```
Sample                      ERIE CANAL
Subject Card  974.7   Adams, Samuel Hopkins
for a book    A            The Erie Canal; illus. by Leonard Vosburgh.
in a series.          N.Y., Random House, 1953.
                          182p. illus. maps. (Landmark Books)
```

Next comes the illustrator's card, and it, too, follows the
same pattern—use the information developed for the basic
unit and add to it, on the first line of the card, the illustrator's name with the notation that he is the illustrator.

```
Sample card                Vosburgh, Leonard, illus.
for illustra-  974.7   Adams, Samuel Hopkins
tor entry for  A           The Erie Canal; illus. by Leonard Vosburgh.
series books.         N.Y. Random House, 1953.
                          182p. illus. maps. (Landmark Books)
```

In each of these examples the series note has appeared in
the collation.

Now we are ready for the series card. Again, the unit developed to describe the book will be used. And, again, the
series note will be included in the collation. The difference
will appear, as is customary, in the first line of the entry.
Here we will place the series title, using lower case lettters.

```
          Landmark Books.                        Sample
974.7    Adams, Samuel Hopkins                   Series entry
A            The Erie Canal; illus. by Leonard Vosburgh.
         N.Y., Random House, 1953.
             182p. illus. map. (Landmark Books)
```

A similar card will be made for every book in the series. The series title will appear on the first line, for these series cards. The information which will follow each such entry, however, will be completely different. Here is another example from the same series for another book.

```
          Landmark Books.                        Sample
92       Kjelgaard, Jim                          Series Entry
M            Explorations of Pere Marquette; illus. by
         Stephen J. Voorhies. N. Y., Random House,
         1951.
             181p. illus. maps. (Landmark Books)
```

Notice also, in the above example, the use of the initial letter of the person who is the subject of the book rather than the initial letter of the author. This, plus the number 92 indicates immediately that this book is a biography, in this case, since we know something of the meaning of this particular series of books, the biography of a man who made a contribution to the growth of the United States.

This book by Kjelgaard would, of course, have its own author entry, its own title entry, probably it would have several subject entries, plus the series entry used above.

Still another kind of added entry card is the card made for a part of a book. This kind of card is called an "analytic" card because it helps to analyze the book. What it does, essentially, is to say: "This part of the book, from page so-and-so to another page so-and-so, is about this topic and it is important enough to call it to your attention."

These analytics ares used, primarily, for books containing short stories which are well-known by title, or plays which are well-known by title, or whole novels which are well-known by title. They may or may not have different authors, and sometimes the authors may be different from the person who was responsible for bringing them together. The analytics are used, also, to point out parts of the book of great significance which might not otherwise be noticed. An example of this might be a book on science which has separate sections on astronomy and physics and chemistry. The title of the book, and the general subject cards for it might not describe these special parts. If the general subject headings do not fulfill this function, then analytics should be used.

The form for analytics is similar to the other added entry forms included in this manual. It does make use of the unit. It does make additional information available on the first line, by inserting a new first line above the unit. This information may be, as we have suggested above, an author's name, a title, or a subject. As is customary, if this entry is an author's name or a title, it will have both upper and lower case letters; if it is a subject it will be in all capital letters. There is one additional characteristic of all analytic cards—they all give the inclusive paging where this added information (in the entry) will be found.

Three examples follow, demonstrating the form for each of these types of analytic cards. It will be important to notice the slight changes in spacing of the entries on the first two lines for the author and title analytics. This is done in order to preserve the "paragraph" form developed for the catalog cards and it enables us to give all the information necessary about the particular part of the book which is being described.

This first example is the author analytic for a very well-known children's play, when this play is one of several in a book and when each has a different author.

```
                Burnett, Frances Hodgson
                Little princess. p.6-15.
822.08   Moses, Montrose J    , ed.
M            A treasury of plays for children; with illus. by
         Tony Sarg. Boston, Little, 1921.
         550p. illus.
```

In this example, a new indention is used for the title of the part of the book which is being presented, but the entry is under the author's name. For this same information to be presented under the title of the play, the form below would be used.

```
                Little princess. p.6-15.
                Burnett, Frances Hodgson
822.08   Moses, Montrose J    , ed.
M            A treasury of plays for children; with illus. by
         Tony Sarg. Boston, Little, 1921.
         550p. illus.
```

In this second example, the title of the part of the book is first because the card will be filed under the title of the play.

When we are not specifying the title of a selection within a book, but need to call attention to a well-known author who may have several selections in the book, we place the

paging note after the author's name and use no analytic titles. Such a card is shown in the following example.

```
                  Shakespeare, William—drama. p.352-75.
822.08            Moses, Montrose J    ʃ ed.
M                     A treasury of plays for children; with illus. by
                  Tony Sarg. Boston, Little, 1921.
                  550p. illus.
```

It is not necessary to include the word "drama" as explanation, but if such an addition assists the user, it may be
desirable to do so.

Subject analytic cards follow the standard form of subject
entries—they make use of all capital letters to indicate the
subject. They also make use of the unit structure. Probably
these are the simplest kinds of analytics to make. An example follows.

```
                  POSTAL SERVICE. p. 255-72.
917.3             Landon, William Chauncy
L                     Everyday things in American life, 1607-1776, N. Y.
                  Scribner, 1937.
                  353p. illus. map. music.
```

It is advisable that whenever a collection and a catalog
have been established, some examination of the forms developed for the various kinds of entries be made before de-
ciding to follow on method rather than another. The forms
given here are fairly well standardized, but many libraries
make adaptations of these forms. Check to see, with inherited catalogs, whether or not a different form has been
developed and is being used. If so, make the necessary
adaptations for continuing to use it.

Cross References

The cross reference card is a sign post which says, "We
do not use the form you are looking under; try this", and

the new directions are given. It may also suggest to the user that there are several other places to look for the material he wants.

The developing of the cross reference cards will require the use of several of the reference books. You will want to use the *Children's Catalog*, the *Basic List* of the A.L.A., and most particularly, the book by Eloise Rue, *Subject Headings for Children's Materials*. As you know from using it in the cataloging process, this consists of a list of subject headings which are practical to use for children's libraries. This list includes not only subject headings to be used as entries, but also those to be used in the card catalog for cross-reference purposes. This book will, later, become a guide for the library and the librarian and a record of what appears in the catalog.

In determining what subject headings to use for books, we use all the materials mentioned above. We will also make use of the alphabetic list found in the *Dewey Decimal Classification and Relative Index*. It is the purpose of cataloging, you will recall, to select headings which will describe the contents of the book. These materials will help us do that and they will also assist in standardizing the headings selected so that they are uniform for any subject.

It is also necessary to take care of another problem. We have to try to anticipate how the user of the library will think about a particular subject and to try to incorporate his particular interpretation of his need into one of these directional sign posts. A sixth grade student, for example, might want to find information about some of the various Indian tribes of the United States. The librarian must anticipate where he will look and guide him to the correct subject headings which are used. And since the librarian cannot, always, be available to work with each child, the headings in the card catalog become an extension of the personal services of the librarian.

It is not always possible to think of every heading which

might be in the mind of all the library's users. The potentialities are too extensive. To help us think wisely and select carefully, we turn to materials which have been developed by others who took considerably more time to think through these problems and who have sifted through the maze of words describing ideas and things and made their work available to us. This is what the book by Eloise Rue provides for us. We will use it in the following ways:

1. to help select the proper form for a subject heading.

2. to compare other possible headings so that a similar form may finally be chosen.

3. to develop a set of headings which are not used so that we may use them as guide posts for the boys and girls. These will then direct them to the proper headings.

This last kind of use assists us in developing the cross-reference cards. These cards are of two basic types—they may be SEE cards or they may be SEE ALSO cards. The SEE card, in effect, tells the user that this heading is not used and tells him where he may find what he needs. The SEE ALSO card tells him that there are other places to look for what he wants and tells him what these places are. Examples of both types are given below.

Example
of a SEE
card

Twain, Mark

see

Clemens, Samuel Langhorne

Example of **a SEE ALSO** **card**	MANNERS AND CUSTOMS see also PEOPLES OF OTHER LANDS

It is important to realize that these simple cards can extend the use of the library immeasurably. And it will be important to keep a permanent record of how the subjects have been selected and what has been selected. Whenever a subject card is typed or prepared for use in the library, that entry should be checked in the list given by Rue. If it is not included in the book, there is space in the column at the right to print the heading opposite the place in the list where it might appear if it had been included. Then, using a pencil, draw a line to the left edge of the printed columns and put an "x" beside the penciled line. These are simple things to do, but they will be important to have for future reference. This kind of checking should be kept up-to-date.

Filing the Cards

The problem of assembling the card catalog can be a very difficult and complicated job. The information below covers only the basic rules and these have been kept fairly simple. Our basic aim is to put together, in one alphabetic arrangement, all of the catalog cards which have been typed for all of the books.

This work may be done as the catalog cards are typed or it may be done as one major phase of the work. For purposes of reference, however, it is most helpful to have the catalog up-to-date with the collection of books as the books are processed.

Begin the work by removing the shelf list cards from the catalog cards if they have been typed at the same time.

Note: Shelf list cards may be identified by the accession numbers which appear on the face of the card.

Since all the cards for all the books will be filed together, it is well to establish some sort of working order.

Sort the cards into piles by the first letter of the first word on the first line of the card. It will not matter if the card is author card or subject card, cross reference or added entry card, since all will be put together in the card file. Omit using the word "a" or the word "the" as the first word in any entry. A card with the first line having the word ASIA would be placed in the A pile. A card with a first line of "A sound in the wind" would go into the S pile. After the piles are established, we must begin to file within the 26 alphabetic letters. Generally, we may use the following set of 12 basic rules. When questions arise which do not seem to be taken care of by one or more of these rules, refer to the book *Rules for Filing Catalog Cards* which has been mentioned earlier.

Filing Rules for Card Catalogs:

1. File each card among the other cards, using the first line of information on the card as the guide.
   Examples: INDIANS OF   file under letter "I"
                 AMERICA
                 An Indian journey   file under letter "A"
                 Isaacson, Peter   file under letter "I"

2. File cards alphabetically by word rather than by letter.
   Examples: Northern passages   Last of the 3 examples.
                 North to the orient   Second in the sequence.
                 North, John R.   First in the sequence.

3. Initials precede a word beginning with the same letters.
   Examples: A N Company   Second in sequence.
                 Anchors aweigh   Third in the sequence.
                 ABC book   First in the sequence.

4. Abbreviations are filed as if they were spelled in full.

    Examples: ICBM   File under: Intercontinental Ballistic Missile

              TVA   File under: Tennessee Valley Authority.

              Mrs.   File under Mistress.

5. Numbers are treated as if they were written in words.

    Examples: 10,000 leagues under the sea. File under: Ten . . .

              54-40 or fight. File under: fifty-four . . .

              1984. File under: Nineteen . . .

6. Omit "the" and "a" in filing if they are the first words. but within a title or subject they are treated as any other word is.

    Examples: The guns of Navarone.   File under: Guns

              In the forest.   File under: In

              Into the forest.   File under: Into. This would follow the 2nd example.

7. If the word "the" or "a" occurs in a foreign language, disregard them as is done in English EXCEPT when they are part of an elision. In that case, file as if they were written in full form. (Note: If in doubt, check with the examples given in the *Rules for Filing Catalog Cards*.)

8. Arrange hyphenated words as separate words.

    Examples: High-buttoned shoes.   First in sequence, entry under *High b*

              Highest buildings   Third in sequence.

              High tower.   Second in sequence, entry under *High t*

9. Names with a prefix are considered as one word. *Mc, M',* and *Mac* are usually filed as if they were all *Mac*. It is acceptable, however, to divide the *Mc* and the *Mac* and to file *M'* with the following word if notation is made in the catalog referring the to the proper place.

    Examples: MacArthur   Usually file under: Maca.

              McOwen   Usually file under: Maco.

              M'Brae   Usually file under: *Macb*.

Note: Use cross reference cards from the form not used to the form used when using any other method. Use either SEE or SEE ALSO cards.

10. If a group of cards have the same first line used as a person, place subject, and title, file them in that order.

Note: This rule applies only when the exact words occur on each of the various cards. When the exact wording is not found on cards, when they only seem to be alike, title by word according to Rule #1.

Example: Jefferson, Thomas.   Speeches.   Last in sequence.
         Jefferson County.   Mississippi.   Second in sequence.
         Jefferson and Lee College.   First in the sequence.

In each case given, the first word is the same, but the second word is not. It is the second word, then, which determines the sequence within the group.

11. Subject cards follow this sequence when the subject heading is the same:
    a. Subject without division.
    b. Subject with form division or sub-subject division.
    c. Subject with time division.
    d. Subject with geographic division.

Note: Subject cards are readily identifiable since they are typed in all capital letters on their first lines.

    Examples: N.Y. STATE—COLONIAL PERIOD-
              1689-1774.   Third.
              N.Y. STATE   First.
              N.Y. STATE—DUCHESS COUNTY.   Last.
              N.Y. STATE. DEPARTMENT
              OF EDUCATION   Second.

12. If the first line of each of several cards is EXACTLY the same, file under the second line within this group, and file the entire group by the first line with the rest of the cards in the catalog.

    Examples: Dickens, Charles.   Oliver Twist.   Second.
              DICKENS, CHARLES.   Last. Use Rule no. 10.
              Dickens, Charles.   Christmas carol.   First.
              Dickens, Charles.   A tale of two cities. Third.

It is always difficult to file without actually handling materials and applying the rules to the work. The following chart puts the rules into practice. The first two lines of a catalog card are given in the first column. For each of these it is necessary to determine the word under which the card is filed first, then the rule (or number of the rule) which covers this particular case, and, last, the place which this item will have in the group of 20 examples given. It is suggested that in this trial run, you cover the last three columns with a sheet of paper on which you may write your own answers and then compare these answers with those given.

FILING QUIZZ

First two lines of catalog card	Word to file under	Special Rule(s) #1 applies to all	Correct Place in this list
a. Shakespeare, William Hamlet	Shakespeare	1	12

b. The PTA in American
   Education
   Crawley, John
	Parent	4	10

c. WASHINGTON, D.C. Smith, John	Washington (a city)	1	19
d. CIO Policies Billings, C. X.	Congress	4	5
e. Three musketeers Dumas, Alexander	Three	1	14
f. Clark, Sonny Playing tennis	Clark	1 & 2	3
g. U.S. Dept. of Agriculture Yearbook	United	4 & 11	16
h. 365 days this year Semain, Leon	Three (number)	5	13
i. Three-phase math. Johnson, Q. R.	Three p	1 & 8	15
j. U.S.–HISTORY Willingworth, Alex	United	4 & 11	17
k. Le petit table. Quentin, X. K.	Petit	7	11
l. Four days U.P.I. and . . .	Four d	1	6
m. MacLyon, Bruce Who goes there?	Mac L	9	9

n. Clarkson, N. Y.			
For all the world	Clarkson	1 & 2	4
o. A-1 Company			
Guide to . . .	A-one	3 & 5	2
p. U.S.–HISTORY–COLONIAL			
Gibson, Marie	United	4 & 11	18
q. The 480			
Burdick, F. S.	Four h	5	7
r. A and N			
Jones, Millicent	A and	3	1
s. McIntosh, Patrick			
Ireland's problems.	MacIntosh	9	8
t. XYZ AFFAIR			
Brown, Charles X.	XYZ	3	20

10

The Shelf List

Function of the Shelf List

The shelf list is used almost exclusively by the librarian or by those who are responsible for the library organization. It is not, in most libraries, even available to the library patrons. It is one of the three major records of the library holdings. Its name describes what it is—namely, a list of the books belonging to the library as they appear on the shelves of the library. Its purpose and its uses relate directly to this characteristic.

Any library needs to have some way of comparing what is actually in the library with what the records show ought to be there. The shelf list is this kind of record—an accurate and up-to-date list of all the holdings of the library. By using it to compare the list of holdings with the materials on the shelf it is possible to take an inventory of the materials and that is one of its functions.

A second major use which the librarian may make of the shelf list is related to the way in which the cards of the shelf list are filed—the classification number arrangement of the shelf list is the only record by subjects. So the librarian, by a skillful but simple procedure, can determine how many titles are available for any classified group. This lets her make a particular use which is most important for school libraries to be able to do. It permits a quick evaluation of the collection, revealing the weak spots and indicating where additional titles are needed to round out and balance the collection.

A third use is to permit the librarian to have available an authoritative list for comparison of contemplated orders against available titles. Such a check before orders are placed will avoid unnecessary or undesirable duplication of titles. It will also assist the librarian in determining when replacements or new editions are needed by having readily available this information about each title. Copyright and publication dates as well as the number of copies of particular titles is a part of the information available.

A fourth use of the shelf list is to help establish and keep available an authoritative form for each author's name. Such information should be included in the shelf list. This kind of information, available so easily, will save many hours of work and will help keep the entry form for each author uniform on all the holdings of the library. This is especially valuable when there may be several acceptable spellings for an author's name or when there is need to know the name under which the books by an author using a pseudonym have been entered.

The shelf list, then, is one of the most important records which will be found in the library. It should be maintained accurately and regularly as materials are added to the library or taken from its collection.

Making Shelf List Cards

In typing the cards for the shelf list, we follow the unit system. That is, the basic information contained on the author card appears in exactly the same format on the shelf list card. The call number appears in the upper left-hand corner. The author's name (or other form for the main entry) is on the first typed line. This is followed by a paragraph containing the imprint—title, joint author, illustrator, or other contributors, edition note, place of publication, publisher, and date of publication. Next comes another paragraph form with the collation—paging, illustration note, series entry.

There are two additional items which are typical of the shelf list card, but which do not appear on the catalog cards. On both printed cards and typed cards it is necessary to add the accession number of the book. If there are several copies of the title or if the title contains several volumes, the accession number for each individual book is given along with its identifying copy number or volume number. The accession number is added below the collation, two typing spaces down, and should begin at the second indention.

The other addition, for specific use on the shelf list card, does appear on the printed cards purchased in sets. It should be added to shelf list cards, both printed and typed. That item is the tracing—the list of subject headings and other entries for which cards are prepared for the card catalog.

If printed cards are being used, it is necessary to identify the shelf list card so that it may have the proper additions placed upon it. The card with the least information on it, the short form, is the shelf list card.

The sample cards which follow show three different kinds of accession entries, each correct for its particular title(s). The first is a sample of the accession entry for one copy of one book. The second is a sample of the shelf list card for one title when several copies are in the collection. The third is a shelf list card on which the accession numbers for several volumes of one title are listed.

| One copy of a title | 522 Schloat, G   Warren
S   Andy's wonderful telescope.   N.Y., Scribner,
          1958.
          48p.   illus.
          689 |

Several copies of one title	K Kipling, Rudyard
	          Puck of Pook's Hill. N.Y., Doubleday, 1946.
	253p. illus.
	          692, c.1
	          693, c.2
	          788, c.3

Several Volumes for one title	R Britannica junior; the boys' and girls' encyclo- 031 paedia; prepared under the supervision of the B the Encyclopaedia Britannica. Chicago, Ency- clopaedia Britannica, 1963. 15 v. illus. maps.

789, v. 1	794, v. 6	799, v. 11
790, v. 2	795, v. 7	800, v. 12
791, v. 3	796, v. 8	801, v. 13
792, v. 4	797, v. 9	802, v. 14
793, v. 5	798, v. 10	803, v. 15

The other item which needs to be added to the shelf list card is the tracing. The example below shows a title which has three such subject headings in the tracing.

Shelf list card with accession no. and tracing	808.88 Belting, Natalia M.
	B The sun is a golden earring; illus. by
	Bernarda Bryson, N. Y., Holt, 1962.
	          n.p. illus.
	          518
	          1. Folklore. 2. Quotations. 3. Universe.

Filing Cards

This file is different from the card catalog and the file
should be kept in its own cabinet or in drawers of the card
catalog separate from the general catalog. As has been
stated earlier, the shelf list is a file of cards arranged as
the books on the shelf are, by classification number.

There may be and usually are several exceptions or some
groups which require a little different handling. Books
which are not going to be circulated from the library are
usually assigned the identifying letter R, standing for the
word "reference", as part of the classification number, pre-
ceding the Dewey decimal number. Shelf list cards for these
books should be put together in a separate section of the
file drawer, just as the reference collection of books will be
separate from the regularly shelved titles. Within the group
of cards for the reference books, the arrangement will be by
classification number.

Another group of cards which are kept together in a separate section of the shelf list are the cards for the fiction
collection. These cards are arranged alphabetically by
author, and within one author's name by book title. This is
the way the fiction books are filed or shelved, so that the
file and the shelving will be alike.

The third group which may be shelved separately and so
will have shelf list cards in a separate section are the books
of individual biography—those numbered 92 or 921 or B
(plus the initial letter of the person about whom the book is
written), depending upon the method used in each particular library. If the 921 number is used for individual biographies, there is no reason for changing the regular sequence
of the books on the shelves. But for the other two codings, it
will avoid confusion to keep the collection of titles, physically, separate from the regular sequence.

With the above special cases in mind, one should first
arrange the shelf list cards into four groups—one for the
reference collection, one for the fiction collection, one for

the individual biography books, and the last group for the regular classification groups. Within all of these groups except the individual biography one, the arrangement is the same—by classification number and after classifiction number alphabetically by author within the grouping. So even though fiction titles will not have numbers, they will fall within this method because the cards will be filed by author and, within author, by title.

Biography cards, individual biography titles, use the initial of the subject of the book, not the author. So, within the number group the author is disregarded and the subject of the book becomes the key for the filing.

The last group of cards, for the general collection, would then be sorted into groups according to the ten major divisions of the classification system—by the hundred number into which they have been placed. After sorting the cards into these smaller groups, take one stack at a time and begin to arrange them numerically by sequence. Do not be confused by the decimal point. Numbers to the right of the decimal point are treated in the same manner as in the regular numbering system—as parts of the whole. The sample below is correct in sequence.

        820.08
        821
        822
        822.08
        822.3
        823
        823.9
        827

Books which have the same classification numbers are shelved in sequence by the author's last name. Shelf list cards use the same method. When the classification numbers are alike, use the author initial or name. When the numbers and the authors names are the same, use the title to complete the alphabetizing.

Three separate sets of examples for the non-fiction groups

and one set for the fiction demonstrate the use of the number and the initials in doing this filing.

Fiction Sequence: If cards for books of fiction include the authors Reese, Marlow, Anderson, Smith, Thomas, Rutland, and Rankin, the correct sequence will be: Anderson, Marlow, Rankin, Reese, Rutland, Smith, Thomas.

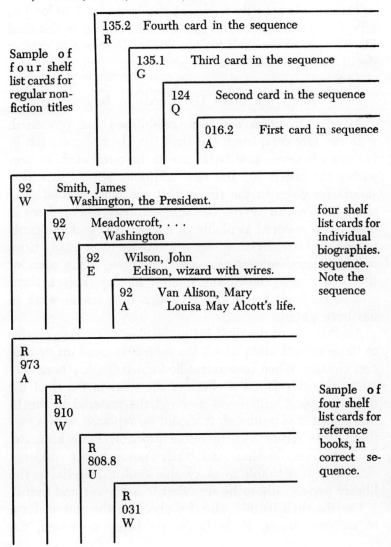

Sample of four shelf list cards for regular non-fiction titles

135.2   Fourth card in the sequence
R

135.1   Third card in the sequence
G

124   Second card in the sequence
Q

016.2   First card in sequence
A

92   Smith, James
W   Washington, the President.

92   Meadowcroft, . . .
W   Washington

92   Wilson, John
E   Edison, wizard with wires.

92   Van Alison, Mary
A   Louisa May Alcott's life.

four shelf list cards for individual biographies. sequence. Note the sequence

R
973
A

R
910
W

R
808.8
U

R
031
W

Sample of four shelf list cards for reference books, in correct sequence.

After the shelf list cards are in proper sequence, it will be helpful to put dividers between the different sections. These dividers may be purchased from library supply houses or from stationery stores or they may be made from cardboard cut to the proper size, with a tab left for indicating the number of the group of cards behind the divider.

These cards actually represent the books, and so long as a book is on the shelf, the cards should remain in the card file. The use of the shelf list file will be described in greater detail in the following sections.

Using the Shelf List Cards in Buying

After a collection has been established and processed, with the files completed, the shelf list file can assist the librarian whenever new books are to be purchased. In preparing the orders for any new additions, special attention should be given to the things that are most needed. The shelf list file can reveal the subject areas where there is little or no material available. A cursory check of the cards behind any one dividing slip will indicate how many titles on the general subject are available. Then, if the users of the library have shown any interest in that subject, there will be verification that this section is or is not as weak as has been stated.

Another use of the shelf list in developing orders pertains to those subject areas which are subject to constant or sudden change. When new scientific knowledge has been discovered or developed, a check of the titles in the shelf list on this subject will reveal how old the material in the library is. If it is outdated, it should be replaced with something more recent and, therefore probably more accurate. As countries develop and their governments undergo change, it is desirable to check this kind of material in the library periodically to be sure that it is current and useful.

Use the shelf list file, also, for checking the correct form of authors' names. If, as books are being processed, the searching for correct names is conducted, the shelf list file will become the authority for any author whose materials are found in the library, and all future entries for this person should conform to the model.

Using the Shelf List for Inventory

The process of inventorying a collection consists of accounting for every book which is supposed to be in the library. If the inventory is taken regularly and the files are revised to conform to the inventory, the library is more useful because the listings of its holdings are accurate. Another major use of the inventory is for the purpose of evaluating the book collection. Only when it is known exactly what a collection contains may it be compared with the standards which compare it with what a satisfactory collection is.

There are also specific conditions which may determine when an inventory should be made. Generally, one may follow these practical guide lines. Inventory should be taken in school libraries when there is a change of administrative personnel, either professional or non-professional. Inventory should also be taken yearly, usually at the end of a fiscal or operating year, both for reporting and for fiscal purposes. Inventory should also be taken whenever there is a set of circumstances which require moving the collection or storing it. Inventories before and after moving it will help safeguard the collection and also the accounting for it. There is apt to be loss of books whenever a collection is moved or when it is placed in storage while building or rehabilitation is under way.

One must prepare to inventory a collection. It is not possible to decide today that in an hour we will begin to inventory a library collection and to start it at that time— not, that is, if we want the work to be accurate and not if we want to do the job with a minimum of wear and tear. Planning must precede the work and certain processes must be completed before the actual inventory can begin.

Libraries are for people to use, and when a library is having extensive use, it is difficult to carry on inventory processes. When it is possible, books should be called back to the library from borrowers and circulation should stop for a brief period. All books should be shelved properly and this requires, then, that the shelves be "read". That is, they must be checked to be certain that each book is in its proper place on the shelf in relation to all other books.

If books cannot be called back to the library, all the book-cards for titles in circulation should be arranged by the Dewey classification numbers (by author for all of the fiction). And the book cards for individual biography titles still in circulation should be arranged properly.

After completing the above steps, the books on the shelves, the book cards for titles still circulating, and the shelf list cards will all be arranged in the same order. In addition to this arranging of all records in an orderly manner, it will be important to have at hand a black pencil, a red pencil, the accession book, a box of paper clips. It will also help to have a typewriter and some blank catalog cards available for use.

The general procedure will be to compare each book on the shelves, in turn, with the shelf list cards in proper sequence. To do this with as little difficulty as possible, it is advisable and desirable that two people work together in the checking process. When this is impossible, one person can handle the job, but it is more awkward and more lengthy with one person than it is with two.

a. General sequence:

1. Begin with the first section of the shelf list.
2. Go to the shelving section where the books listed in this section of the shelf list are found.
3. Read the author and title on the first shelf list card.
4. Compare it with the author and title of the first book on the shelf.

5. If they correspond, move along to the second card and the second book.

6. Continue this sequence through the entire collection.

b. Handling Irregularities in the General Sequence:

1. When books are out of place, remove them. Take time, later, or have a second person, to place them in their proper location on the shelves.

2. When books are missing, put a paper clip on the shelf list card and move along to the next card and the next book.

3. When there are MULTIPLE COPIES of books, it is necessary to compare the copy numbers and the accession numbers of all the copies with the listings on the shelf list. If any copy is missing, check the proper accession number with the black pencil on the shelf list card, put a paper clip on the card, and move along to the next title.

4. When the book is in the proper place, but when there is no shelf list card, tip the book on the shelf or tag it with a strip of colored paper. Do not remove it. Cards for the shelf list can be made at this time or they must be made later, depending on the available help. It is advisable to do this as quickly as possible.

5. If shelf list cards are to be made, it is advisable to check the card catalog under the author and title entries to see if the shelf list card was incorrectly filed in the card catalog and to verify whether or not any catalog entries were made for the book. If the shelf list card was misfiled, remove it and file it properly in the shelf list file. If no cards for the book are found in the card catalog, make a work card for the book and type the complete set of catalog cards and the shelf list card as promptly as possible.

c. Reconciling All Records of the Library Collection

1. After the collection has been checked, books which were removed because they were out of a place should be compared with the shelf list and then put back on the shelves in the proper place. If a paper clip was used to tag the shelf list card (to indicate a missing title), remove the clip. If the book is one of several copies and the accession number was checked, erase the check.

2. Compare the BOOK CARDS for books still in circulation with the shelf list cards marked with paper clips and remove the paper clip if the book is accounted for in the circulation records.

3. All shelf list cards for missing books should be marked in black pencil with the words: missing, and the date. This should be written in very small script and should be directly opposite the

accession number. If there are multiple copies of the books and if only some of the copies are missing, make this notation opposite the accession numbers which were checked in pencil when the first checking was done.

4. Mark the accession record also, using the same wording to indicate the date on which the book was discovered to be missing, opposite the entry for the book. Be sure that the accession number on the shelf list card is identical with the number of the accession record and the entry in the accession record. DO THIS WITH RED PENCIL.

5. Type a list of all missing titles, giving 3 items of information about each: accession number, author, and title.

6. This list should be filed with the individual to whom you are responsible—the person who cleared the way for you to work in the library.

d. Follow-Up:

1. As time permits, it is desirable that a further check be made of the books found to be missing in this inventory. It is possible that the titles were misplaced.

2. Publicize among the borrowers and users of the library the titles which are missing. It is possible that some titles were inadvertently taken from the library without being properly checked out.

e. Clearing the Shelf List and the Card Catalog: After is seems certain that the missing materials will not be found, the shelf list and the catalog will have to be corrected to take care of maintaining an accurate listing.

1. If there is only one copy of the book listed on the shelf list card and if this copy is missing, remove the shelf list card from the file.

2. If there are several copies of the book and only some of them are missing, mark the missing copies (by comparing the accession numbers in the book with those on the shelf list card) but retain the cards in the files.

3. If the shelf list card is removed, the card catalog will also have to be cleared. The tracing on the shelf list card will tell what the catalog entries for this title are. Check the card catalog for the author entry, the title entry, and for any other entries indicated on the shelf list card. As the catalog cards are found, staple them to the shelf list card and file them in some accessible spot.

4. Retain these files of cards for one year to allow time for lost

materials to reappear. If they do not appear, at the beginning of the next inventory discard the file of cards for these missing books.

This final discard of the shelf list materials for a book completes the inventory procedures. It is possible that between inventories, however, some of this record-keeping for a collection will be necessary, but with only one or two titles at a time in all probability. Such constant revision of the records of the holdings is normal, and makes the large inventory sessions less strenuous.

11

Shelving The Books

Sorting the Collection and Allocating Space

When books have been completely processed and are ready for shelving, it is important to stop for a moment and do some planning. By now it will be obvious that there are a certain number of books which will have to be placed in certain areas, but some determination will have to be made as to what will go into each of these areas.

Books are shelved by classification numbers. This means that it will be helpful to sort the books into piles by these classification numbers. This can be done at the time the books are being processed. One of the simplest ways to do this sorting is to have several boxes available into which the books are put as they are processed. Each of these boxes can be for a specific classification group, if there is a large quantity of books being handled. Or, for smaller groups of books it may be as efficient to group two or three number sequences together.

Fiction should be sorted at this time and kept separate from all non-fiction. And individual biographies should be separated, also, from the general non-fiction collection at this time. These two groups are handled, in shelf arrangement, a bit differently from other books. One other group should be set off—the collection of reference books, identified by the use of the letter R above the call number.

After this dividing of the collection has been completed, it is well to use the shelf list cards, now in order, to see how many books of each classified group there are. Write these figures down, thus, for you will want to refer to them very soon:

Fiction 1698	000 — 9	500 — 218
Reference 112	100 — 3	600 — 87
Individual Biography 197	200 — 2	700 — 63
Collected Biography 211	300 — 311	800 — 75
	400 — 19	900 — 187

These figures, giving the quantity of books in each category will help you in working out the space allocation.

The reference collection should be housed near the charging desk or near the place where the librarian will be doing most of her work. The fiction should be housed in an area large enough to take the entire collection in sequence with very few breaks in the sequence. This is true, also, for the individual biography collection. The collected biographies may be shelved in numerical sequence with the other books. All other books may be shelved in sequences by number, but without whole sections as divisions.

Space should be so allocated that each of these groupings can be taken care of. To do this, for children's books (except reference) we usually allow for about 12 titles for each running foot of shelf space. If books are very thin, a foot may accommodate more. If books are very big, a foot will not take this many. But, by comparing the approximate number of feet required for each group, using the working list you have developed as above, with the number of feet available in each section of the library, it will be possible to make some reasonable decisions about where the books are going to be housed.

For the reference collection it is more practical to allow only 8 books to each foot of running space since encyclope-

dias are larger than average books and since other reference
books may also require more space.

Having made the estimate of the number of feet required
for each group, and having examined the shelf areas to see
how they provide the proper amount of space for each
group, it is important to move the stacks of piled books into
the approximate areas where they will, eventually, be
placed.

It is preferable not to put them upright on the shelves,
although to place them in piles on the shelves in the proper
areas will not be confusing. After the books have been
moved into the area, our next step is to shelve them.

Shelving Procedures

a. Reference Collection: The reference collection is shelved
exactly as the non-fiction collection—by classification number and, within classification number groups which are
alike, by author's last name.

b. General Non-Fiction Collection: Shelve these books by
classification numbers and, within classification number
groups, by author's last name. Begin in both this section and
the reference collection section with the 000 group and
progress from left to right through the 900 section.

c. Individual Biography Collection: These books are
shelved all within the general classification number used
for this group (92 or 921 or B), alphabetically by the last
name of the person about whom the book is written. A book
about George Washington by someone named Smith would
have the number W92 or the number W921 or the number
WB. In all of these cases, the book would be filed under
the word WASHINGTON within the numbered group.
Books about people whose names begin with A would come
first; those whose names begin with Z would come last.

d. The Fiction Collection: Books of fiction are classified
only by the author's initial letter, as described in chapter
VII. This means that books will have to be arranged accord-

ing to the last name of the author—alphabetically—within this fiction group. If there are many books of fiction, it will be well to separate the collection along the shelves by the letters of the alphabet and then to compare the names of the authors of the books within each letter's group. This will require care in checking each name of each author against the books which come before and after it. But taken one at a time, checked one at a time, and arranged one at a time, the work moves surprisingly fast.

e. General Shelving Sequence: In the United States and in other countries where the movement of the eyes in reading is from left to right, the shelving sequence used will seem logical. For books, too, move from left to right, with smaller classification numbers being placed there and the larger ones coming, logically farther to the right. This sequence moves downward, also, through the shelves. Perhaps the small diagram below will illustrate better than words.

Begin here. Continue in this direction→ then come
down to this spot and continue in sequence→

f. Shelf Labels: It will be helpful to type or letter the general headings for each of the Dewey classification divisions on cardboard and fasten these signs to the proper shelves. These will be signposts for the boys and girls using the library and will help them find their way around.

g. Inventory: After a collection is processed, and before it is allowed to circulate, inventory should be made to be sure that records are in order with the collections. See Chapter X for the proper method and proper sequence to follow.

12

Maintaining The Collection

Weeding and Discarding

Children's libraries are not archives or storehouses. They are functional laboratories for learning and for leisure reading activities. As times change, as society changes, so, too, do the needs of these libraries. It is not enough to have a group of books. The books must be the right ones. There is constant need to see that materials which have outlived their usefulness, materials which are out of date, materials which are falling apart are weeded from the collection.

Some of the guidelines for selecting books to weed from the collection are:

1. Discard books which are physically worn out. Badly torn covers; pages too soiled or too yellowed to clean; many pages torn or missing from the book—these are conditions which cannot be taken care of easily. If the content is still useful, replacement is the only way to handle this.

2. When the contents are loose in the cover, and when the stitching of the sections of the book is loose, discard.

3. When the information in the book is out-of-date, discard.

4. When the format of the book is a deterrent to its use, discard. A good example of this, unfortunately, is the edition of children's classics which has such small print, or which has such narrow margins that it the book will not appeal to young people.

5. Discard, also, books which should never have been in a children's library—titles which are completely unsuitable. These might be the old textbook or the adult book; they might be the cheaply made and poorly written books; they might be books which have been sitting on the shelves for several years with no use.

There are several steps to be taken in handling the discards. After the books for discard have been selected, take them from the shelves, removing the book card from the pocket of each book. Pack the books in boxes and report to the individual in charge what you are prepared to discard (a typed list of titles and authors) and why these materials should be discarded.

Using the book cards, find the entry for the book in the accession record and clear this record by drawing a red line through the accession entry and writing the word "DIS-CARDED" with the date of discard in the remarks column of the accession record. Next clear the shelf list record and the card catalog. For these last two processes, refer to the last section of the previous chapter. The method used for clearing these records for discarded materials is the same method described for clearing the records for lost books.

Mending

Books which are fairly new, attractive, and only lightly soiled may be mended—provided that supplies for mending are available and providing that there is plenty of time. Library supply houses sell mending supplies and most of them also will issue a pamphlet describing mending procedures. They also pack supplies into "kits" which include some of each of the basic materials necessary to carry out a mending program, but not a tremendous quantity of them.

Because the mending process is very complicated, it is advisable to consult one of the booklets available from the supply firms, follow the instructions in it step-by-step, using the materials described in the booklet.

If time is at a premium, it may be more desirable to discard books and to purchase new copies that it will be to mend. Or, if the book is worth saving, it may be more economical to have the book rebound by a rebinding company.

If you decide to mend, be prepared to contribute endless hours to an older collection. But weigh the values against the problems. Who knows what you will discover in your particular case?

Guarding Against Deterioration

Preventive care of books, like preventive medicine, is more to be desired than curing the problem. And, having gone to extensive work to establish a library, we should be interested in knowing how to take care of it. There are many factors involved in the care of books, some within our ability to control and others far beyond it.

Perhaps the care of books begins with the making of the book. The kind of paper, the kind of ink, the kind of binding —these we cannot change and these we take as they come. Neither can we change the basic climate of the locality in which we live. Yet all of these items determine, in part, whether or not the book or other library materials will last. In most instances, however, there are steps to take which can extend the life of the book beyond what it would normally be if we did nothing.

The whole problem of safeguarding books—especially for large libraries with extensive collections and with very precious and old books—is a fascinating one, and one which is being studied very seriously. The National Archives in Washington, D. C., the British Museum in London, England, the Instituto di Patologia del Libro in Rome, Italy, and UNESCO have all been involved in scientific research dealing with the problem. This has been concerned with the materials from which books are made, the effect of various kinds of climate on these materials, the insect and plant life which threaten to destroy books, and the atmospheric and chemical conditions which create damage.

Our concerns will be simpler. And we will assume that our books, since they are to be used, will eventually wear out after a normal life, and will, in due time, be discarded and replaced. We will not be trying to keep books on our shelves for twenty or thirty years, for children's libraries are not archives. But the book should live its normal life, and for that length of time—different as this may be for each book—we want to take care of the materials.

The way in which the book is shelved may affect the condition of the book. To give it the greatest possible life span, shelve a book so that it stands upright. On the shelf, books should be firmly held in place, but not so tightly that it is impossible to move them. Small spaces between the books will allow air to circulate around the books, and this is desirable. Books should not be shelved so loosely that they sag nor so tightly that they are squeezed together. Sagging may pull the contents out of the binding. It will most certainly create a strain on the binding. Use book ends to give the desired amount of firmness.

Do not tip a book so that it faces downward. To do so will cause the contents to pull on the binding and, eventually, to tear the edges of the binding.

Large books should be placed upright in shelf space prepared to take large books. If books are very heavy, they should be placed flat on a shelf with the spine of the book facing outward. Avoid piling many heavy books together, for the book at the bottom will take the weight of all the books on top.

If it is necessary to move books, every precaution should be taken to avoid dropping the books. The sewing, the gluing, the covers, the pages—all these parts of the book take the strain when it is dropped, and no book is so firmly bound or put together that it cannot be damaged. Pages can be torn, covers can be ripped, corners can be bent, and the contents may come loose from the book under such strain.

When books are removed from a shelf, the fingers should

be slipped into the space between this book and the neighboring books, with the thumb to the back of the book and the fingers to the front, near the top of the binding. Then the book should be gently swung forward without tipping it back on the lower edge of the binding. Avoid pulling the book out of its place by tugging on the rather fragile cloth which forms the spine of the book.

How many books should be carried at once? There is no one answer for everyone, but generally carry only enough to be comfortable. Never try to carry so many books that you feel you must strain to reach your destination safely. It is easier on you and on the books to make two trips or to get help. Book trucks, too, can save wear and tear on the librarian as well as on the books.

Cleanliness, for books, is as important as cleanliness for people. Aside from any distaste which comes from handling and using soiled books, dirt of any kind constitutes a real hazard to the books. If the bindings are particularly valuable, for example, dust particles can scratch leather or parchment, and thus destroy a protective coating. On books of lesser value, as well as on rare items, dust absorbs moisture and, in time, can dry the moisture out of the pages. The result is brittle paper, which results, in turn, in pages which tear easily. Pages also discolor with dust. Another dirt hazard is the oily and greasy dirt which are found commonly in large cities. These are substances which attract insects and rodents. Even on new books, soil can attract insects and mice—and both insects and mice are creatures which gnaw. Cleanliness will pay—literally. Vacuum cleaning is the least likely to create damage in books as a cleaning medium. Any library would do well to vacuum its books once a year.

Where we choose to shelve the books will also help preserve the collection or contribute to an earlier demise. Direct sunlight, heat from radiators, or hot currents of air should not be allowed to touch the shelves. This is especially true if the shelving is metal rather than wood. Metal will conduct and store heat and cause both the binding and the pages, as well as the adhesives, to dry and become brittle. Moisture, too, is one of the elements to guard against. It can be as damaging as heat. Steam from radiators, leakage from pipes, dampness from seepage into the shelving area can loosen paste, stretch sewing, and cause complete disintegration of books.

During a week of displaying an extensive book exhibit, it was the author's misfortune to have a violent rain storm with winds arise over a week-end. So violent was the wind that it blew the rain into the weakened mortar on the outside of the building. When Monday morning came, after this Sunday storm, an examination of the room showed that one entire table of books had been exposed to its own little private cascade of water, and some fifty books had, quite literally, disintegrated. Covers were loose from the books and loose from the binding boards. Thread, used in sewing the collections of pages together for a book, was so stretched that the sections could be extended a good half-inch from each other. Rarely does this extreme damage occur without flood, but it can.

You know the expression: "It isn't the heat; it's the humidity." Most people use it to describe their own discomforts in hot weather. If books could talk, they, too, might use the expression. But they would refer to the persistent kind of humidity which is found in many climates and, sometimes in particular rooms of buildings. Temperature and humdity do, indeed, need to be controlled to help take care of books. If the temperature ranges beyond the 65°-70° span with humidity outside the 50%-60% range, there is a serious problem. If the air contains noxious fumes of any sort—gas, manufacturing plant fumes, the famous "smog" of certain localities—these are potential dangers. Chemical residue in the air is as bad for books as it is for people. And books are probably as susceptible to drastic changes in temperatures and humidity levels as people are, even though books and people do not always agree on the same temperatures and moisture content for their atmospheres.

There are special kinds of hazards to guard against in each different locality. Mildew can create serious damage in books. It usually develops when dampness and high temperature occur together. Try, if this kind of climate exists for the books, to prevent its forming. Create dry air if possible and control the heat. Air conditioning will do this. Or create dry air temporarily by using dehumidifiers or chemicals which absorb moisture, dry each book individually, and lacquer the cover after a good drying. This may help prevent the formation of mildew.

Molds of various sorts may develop and live under the same conditions as mildew or they may be more comfortable living in other climates. Again, seek to prevent their development by creating a "hostile" environment—the kind of temperature and humidity and general environment which discourages the growth of the molds. Preventive measures are apt to be more effective than curative measures. Fumigation may have to be resorted to. This is a complicated and time-consuming process. It also requires placing the materials in air-tight compartments, subjecting them to the chemical fumes, and letting them stay undisturbed until the fumigation has been completed. Then there must be care in opening and in handling the materials, avoiding contamination from the chemicals and avoiding contaminating the materials again. If it is necessary to undertake this measure, it is advisable to consult with someone who has been through this process or to employ an expert.

Do you have pests? In some parts of the United States and in many of the tropical and subtropical climates termites constitute a threat to books. According to those who have studied this problem extensively, the termite actually lives in wood, eating wood fibers. And since paper is, frequently, made of wood fiber, this can be an attractive substance to these pests. This is a problem left better to special companies whose work it is to exterminate termites rather than to the amateur. In the Far East, termites are one of the major hazards to books. The Imperial Department of Agriculture in India and the Imperial College of Tropical Agriculture, too, have developed formulae to be used in insecticides for these and other typical pests. It is reported that the use of naphelene balls, camphor, or raw lime cakes will act as a deterrent not only to termites, but also to moths, silverfish, beetles, and cockroaches. These chemicals are placed on the shelves in the areas where the insects are prevalent and also where they are apt to be found. It is recommended that in establishing a library in an area where there is any indication that these insects might appear, a check be made with the company installing the library shelving to see if they can use a varnish formula which incorporates an insect repellent. It is much better to try to avoid having an environment attractive to these creatures and to prevent their finding a breeding place with the books than it is to try to get rid of them after playing the gracious host to them.

Another kind of pest is the cockroach. It is so obnoxious a creature that it deserves special mention. Mr. Minendra Basu, in his small pamphlet on *Library and Preservation* indicates that borax, sprinkled on book shelves, will deter cockroaches, and states, further, that it is a specific against them.

It is interesting to note that it is the nature of certain materials to be subject to certain reactions to environmental factors. Basically, preservation consists either of controlling the environmental factors by eliminating the dangerous elements in it or by keeping them from behaving as they normally would when they come in contact with the paper, cloth, glues, paste, etc. which comprise the book.

All kinds of materials face various kinds of threats. It is normal to expect ordinary materials to wear out after sufficient use. But when the environment does not permit the materials to live their normal lives, then it is important to control the enemies of the materials.

Extensive studies are being conducted by various companies to determine not only how to safeguard books, but also how to store valuable materials which cannot be replaced. Most small libraries do not have this kind of problem. Occasionally, however, authors' autographs or an original illustration or a page of manuscript may be a gift to a library. Flat pages of this kind may be preserved in several ways. Two which are within the budgets and capabilities of small libraries are: 1. laminate the page between sheets of plastic, and 2. frame the page, putting it behind glass after mounting it. Either method calls for a professional job to be done by an expert.

13

Housing and Equipping the Library

Space Needs

Books may be housed in many different kinds of space, and boys and girls may try to make use of them in these various places. Collections of books have been housed in buildings of various kinds and in various parts of buildings—they have been shelved in hallways, in closets, in small rooms, in large rooms, in classrooms, in auditoriums, in cafeterias, in gymnasiums. They have also been housed on wheels—small book carts, especially planned automobile or jeep or truck facilities, improvised shelves mounted on rollers. And books have been shelved in boxes, on planks, on tables, on floors.

Improvising library facilities and improvising housing space for libraries may be necessary. When this is the case, such improvising should be done with the broadest possible kind of imaginative approach to try to project into this planning the greatest possible scope for the development of the space and its faciliteis. In truth, libraries are and represent th wide expanse of man's intellectual development and his knowledge of himself and the universes. Every effort should

159

be made to let the library reflect the best of that development and the best of the cultural life of the community—whatever it may be. There is a responsibility inherent in the idea of a library to let his intellectual heritage be absorbed by the people who come to the library, and to let them grow into the appreciation of the best of all man's efforts.

If there is little money, if there are few facilities, if there is little help, more must be done by those interested to make what there is better than one has a right to expect it to be. It is one of the characteristics of societies which are changing rapidly and growing rapidly, that the people learn ingenuity—they learn how to make the best of whatever they have, they learn how to improvise for improvement, and they reach toward something better. These are all attributes which can be put to excellent use when working with less than desirable library facilities.

There is nothing "wrong" in not having the best. There is an obligation, however, to try to make things better. The recommendations which follow try to present several different kinds of situations and to indicate how each could be planned to allow the kind of library program to function as it is considered desirable.

a. Planning School Libraries for Children. If it is possible to select space or to build space for a library in a school, this planning should include some thought about how the library is going to be used, what the aims of the services are, how many children will be using this library, any special kinds of program in the school, the ages of the children, the locality in which the school is located, how many books will be purchased or are already available, whether or not materials other than books are a part of the collection.

If some generally accepted basic items can be mentioned, which apply to all situations, we can then develop the areas of differences which may exist in the various kinds of situations.

Most authorities would agree that children's libraries should be light and airy and cheerful. This means that regardless of whether the space is to be built or if it already exists, it should have these characteristics. It should provide enough space for whatever uses the library will be put to. If the library is to be used for quiet, individual reading, for instance, it will not be necessary to have as much space as would be needed for both large and small group work involving many different kinds of learning materials such as filmstrips and recordings and models and exhibit materials. The library should provide, it follows, for the housing of the various kinds of materials which will be part of its collections. Books require one kind of space; maps require another; and the newer materials of transparency projection and sound reproduction and cross media require both more and different kinds of space.

Generally, too, it will be agreed that the atmosphere of the library should be warm and welcoming, but non-violent. Colors should enhance the attractiveness and should be in keeping with good taste.

Let us examine the above and try to be more helpful in giving specific information. Space, for example, should be related to: a. library services, b. library collection, c. school enrollments, d. school program. If the library services are limited to individual use rather than group or class use, less space is needed. If the library collection houses only books and if it never will include any other kind of materials, the amount and kind of space needed will be different from that needed if many different kinds of materials were to be housed in this area. If school enrollments are kept to a specific number, and if no expansion of the kinds of groups of students is expected, the space will be quite different from what would be needed if physically handicapped children, using wheel chairs or using braille materials or using special recordings for the deaf or special visual materials, requiring special equipment and special facilities, were to be a part of the group of students who formed the school.

Generally, for research and reference and reading purposes, one child will need an allowance of no less than 25 square feet. This provides space for his movement, his materials, his table and chair. Whenever anything additional is added—other materials, other functions, special programs —it is necessary to allow more space per child. The 25 square feet may be called the minimum figure. The next factor is the number of students who should be expected to use the library at one time. Again, for most school situations, it should be expected that entire classes will come at one time to the library, and so seating should be provided (seating plus the table space) to allow for the largest class in the school to come to the library.

If a school also permits students from other classes to be in the library with the class group, additional space is needed for this part of the program up to the proper number of square feet for the number of students to be allowed to use the library at one time.

Another way to compute the minimum size needed for a children's school library is to assume that one tenth of all the students may come to the room at any one time. A school with 300 students would plan for a library which would accommodate 30 students. A school with 600 students would plan for a library to accommodate 60 students. But, again, if the use is to be limited, the size of the library may be smaller.

If the library is to provide, also, audiovisual materials (such as slides, film-strips, and recordings) additional space will be needed so that the necessary equipment can be accommodated. The amount of space will depend upon the number of units of each kind which might be available for use at one time. If this equipment is to be used by a group as well as by an individual, some additional, especially equipped space may be needed to provide light-control facilities or special electrical facilities or special kinds of seating.

With a variety of equipment and materials, too, storage space and work space will need to be increased. Equipment will require space for repair and maintenance as will the materials. Tapes and filmstrips need to be examined for damage, spliced as necessary, and stored properly. Each kind of material will require additional space and space of a particular kind.

It is necessary for the librarian, either professional or non-professional, to have space to work. Logically such space should be a part of the library. To do the mechanical and professional and technical work of the librarian, there will need to be desk and shelf space, cupboard space, a sink, closet space, and space for any special files. These are basic. Additionàl space will provide for additional functions.

All of these kinds of space may be translated into different kinds of arrangement. The arrangements depend upon the whole and large area set aside for this purpose.

b. Locating the Library. During the past ten years, it has been a common problem that education must run to keep pace with knowledge. It is this kind of educational problem which libraries help solve. But to help solve it, something must, first, go into the libraries. Books, yes. But also certain kinds of space.

In planning new buildings, perhaps the most dangerous type of planning is to arrive at a "set" program, a "set" space, with "set" facilities. Change is in the air of education, and the adaptability of space and facilities may be the factor which lets the curriculum grow and expand. So the library, that central area from which the intellectual and learning movement of the school can emanate, must be planned to allow for the growth and change. Expansion must be built into it.

Walls can be removed for expansion if they are built with that in mind. If heavy-duty wiring is a part of the school's installations, outlets can be strategically placed at intervals to allow for any future contingency by the removal of small metal plates. Or conduits can be installed to take wiring, with easy access to permit later necessary installations.

But when a room is placed between solid, immovable walls, between walls containing the permanent plumbing systems and permanent electrical systems, or, in some places, gas and oil systems, it is almost impossible to bring about any extension of space. This kind of location for the library should be avoided at all costs.

In schools, too, where students make extensive use of the library, it should be so placed that it is accessible to the students. Schools with one building may center the library vertically and horizontally or may place it near a bank of classrooms or a cluster of rooms where the subject assignments will require ready access to the materials of the library. Sometime libraries are placed in the center of a circle of classrooms with access from two or three or four floors to this center. Schools with several buildings may find that the library is most useful when it is a separate and central building with space around it for the addition of facilities as the school may grow.

Whatever the solution and the decision, it is essential that some far-sighted planning precede the final acceptance of plans. Library authorities can and should be consulted. Suggestions given in the early chapters for those who can give advice on work and organizational procedures may be put to good use in this area, too. If a building is to exist and to serve any group of a community for several generations, it should be planned with a look as far into the future as it is possible to see. And when vision lags, the expert may be able to extend the vision with some high-powered time-glasses for our mental eyes.

c. The Library Atmosphere. To help create the atmosphere of warmth and light and welcome which has been mentioned, it might be well to add a few words of caution.

Avoid, in paint or finishing enamels, colors so garish that they are out-of-keeping with the cultural image you wish to present. Let the room be livable. Provide for both light and light control. Reading in direct sunlight is not a good educational experience. Be sure that the temperature of the room can be comfortable at all times. Windows should not admit rain, even under the most severe storm conditions which are typical of the area. Or, for a desert country, substitute "sand" or "dust" for the word "rain".

Some acoustical control should be built into the library structure. Ceilings or wall areas or floors, both in materials and in finishes, should help control the reverberation of sound. Remember that hard surfaces reflect sound, and that sound waves may bounce back and forth several times in a room before they are dispersed unless something absorbs them. Garbled sound or sound which carries and cannot be understood mean that the control is poor. An easy test of the quality of control is to clap your hands and as you clap them begin to count. If you count as far as four or five before the sound has disappeared, the room presents acoustical problems.

Safety exists are required by most cities' building codes or by most state education departments or by the authorities approving building plans in any area. It is well to ask questions concerning the planning for safety as it relates to any normal hazards.

From time to time there has been mention here of the role of the library in representing a "cultural" level which is a model for the young people using the library to learn from. There are several ways in which behavioral patterns may be controlled and changed by the type of library furnishings and facilities provided. The use of carpeting on the floor is one. No, it is not difficult to take care of nor will it wear out before a tile floor. New materials make carpeting practical and comparably economic as floor finishes. Behavior changes are noticeable, too, and indicate that the kind of room that is created can affect the behavior of people. The addition of some informally arranged easy chairs or living-room type furniture can also change behavior patterns. These ideas may be interesting or not, but it might be important to test them for oneself.

Furniture

Tables and chairs are the beginnings of furniture. Buy them in appropriate sizes for those who will use them. Certainly tables and chairs for children should not be of the same height as those for adults. Furniture companies frequently standardize the heights of tables and chairs, and catalogs of the manufacturers of library furniture reflect these differences.

One of the major furniture needs is shelving. The kind of shelf space which will be needed will depend upon the materials. If all shelving is adjustable, that is, if the shelves may be placed at different heights in the casings, it is less difficult to adapt the shelving to the collection. Certain kinds of materials, however, call for special shelving characteristics. Very large books, such as are made for the younger children, require wider shelf space as well as deeper shelf space. The deeper shelf space can be provided by having adjustable shelves, but the wider shelf space must be purchased in the proper width. So, too, films will require special shelving racks, preferrably of steel, since film is very heavy and needs sturdy support. Disc recordings, too, will require special shelving.

It would be practical to learn whether or not, when money is not available readily, it is possible to have shelves built for certain parts of the library. If it is, these should be equipped with the metal strips which permit that the shelves be adjusted. Fixed shelving and shelving of the wrong size can easily become useless shelving.

Other items of furniture which are basic to the proper

functioning of the library include the card catalog units and the vertical files. The card catalog unit will house the card catalog and, possible, the shelf list. As has been noted in earlier chapters, these are indispensable for a real library and should be considered first purchase. Under only the most desperate circumstances should these be made locally. It is possible to improvise with whatever is at hand for other furniture needs, but not for the card catalog cabinet. It is better to use the heavy cardboard files which are available from the library supply houses, and which are made to house the cards properly, than it is to try to use ordinary boxes. Money may not permit the purchasing of a good wooden or metal cabinet, but this is one item of furniture which should be considered as worthy of early purchase.

Other furniture which is needed, which can be purchased also or for which some substitutes can be found when funds are not available for purchase, include: stands for large unabridged dictionaries, stands for large map books, magazine racks, book trucks, bulletin boards, a desk for the librarian with charging tray, swivel chair, wastebaskets.

The amount and kind of furniture which should be purchased is controlled by the amount of money available, the plans for further development of the library, the number of children who will use the library, the space available, the interest of the library's administrative officers. Whenever it is impossible to provide complete facilities, it is advisable to plan over a period of years to work toward something which is acceptable and which, year by year, can reflect the improvement.

Some of the manufacturers of standard library furniture are listed on the following page. Many of these companies have representatives in various parts of the United States and make the advisory services of these representatives available to schools and other institutions on request. Such services center about the development of physical facilities of libraries and, as should be expected, the proper equipment for them. One can learn a great deal from such assistance and from the kind of advice which will help develop a long-time plan for growth.

Manufacturers of Library Furniture In The
United States of America

Art Metal Construction Co.
Jamestown, New York

Beckley-Cardy Co.
1900 North Narragansett
Chicago, Illinois, 60639

Brod-Art
56 Earl Street
Newark 14, New Jersey

C.A. Colligan Co.
945 Front Street
Uniondale, Long Island, N.Y.

Delux Metal Furniture Co.
Warren, Pennsylvania

Fordham Equipment Co.
2377-79 Hoffman Street
New York 58, New York

Worden Co.
Holland, Michigan

Library Bureau of Remington Rand
122 East 42nd Street
New York 17, New York

Myrtle Desk Co.
High Point,
North Carolina

Royal Metal Manufacturing Co.
175 North Michigan Avenue
Chicago 1, Illinois

John E. Sjoutrom Co.
1717 North Tenth Street
Philadelphia, Pennsylvania

Standard Wood Co.
Coliseum Tower
10 Columbus Circle
New York 19, New York

Walker Bilt Co.
Penn Yan, New York

The Library Which Travels

In addition to libraries which are housed in particular rooms of particular buildings, there are many uses for liraries on wheels—both short and long distances.

Short-distance mobile libraries may be part of a school, a hospital, some other institution or business—almost any type of organization which makes any use of a library can make some use of the small collection on wheels. In schools, for instance, when individual classroom collections are desired for special use within the classroom, it is helpful to be able to put a selected collection of pertinent materials on a book truck and move the collection from the library into the classroom. Then, when the materials have served their purpose, the collection can be moved back to the library with a minimum of effort.

Sometimes the manufactured book truck is not available. Improvised trucks may be put together using boxes such as milk lugs. The sketch of the milk lugs which follows was made from a set of such book trucks developed for use in a school which needed mobility for its book collection. These were painted bright pastel colors by the children of the school so that they, too, participated in helping equip their school's library.

If lumber, screws, and the necessary tools are available, it is possible for other mobile units to be made. Skill with the tools will result in a better looking book truck, but even irregularities in minor places need not keep one from having a functional method of moving books.

If books have to be carried by hand a single shelf, with a handle on the top and a strap to keep the books from sliding out of the shelves, can be made in a size suitable for the particular use it will be put to and suitable for carrying under different kinds of circumstances. This single shelf may, also, be used for display purposes. Place it on a table, remove the strap, and the hand-truck becomes a shelf to show off the books.

Another kind of movable shelf, but one which takes a bit more doing, may be made of bricks (ceramic or glass) to be used as the uprights between the shelves and boards or plastic sheets as the shelf area. This kind of shelf can be taken down, transported to where it will be used, and there reassembled. It is a bit awkward to handle in this way, but possible if there are no other facilities available.

Then there are the professional mobile library facilities—or, indeed, whole libraries. These are lumped together under the name, "Bookmobile", but the name only begins to

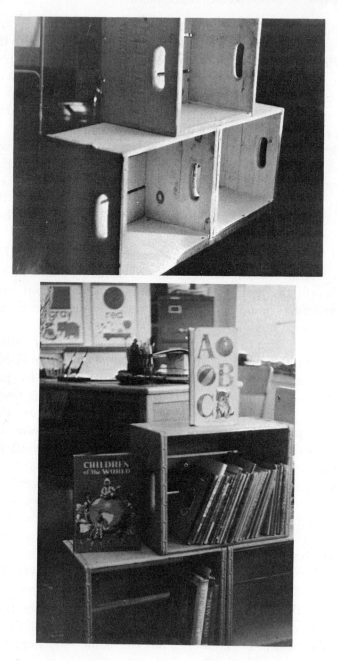

describe what they are and what they can provide. Usually the bookmobile is an adjunct of a library large enough and well-enough stocked with materials and with sufficient professional staff to actually move a part of its collection and its staff out of the central library to a remote spot where library services are not available. In large cities of the United States, in remote country areas, in newly developing nations, in any place at all where it is possible to travel by land, bookmobiles may be found.

These vary from large and well-equipped trailer-type autotrucks to smaller or "jeep-sized" facilities. Regardless of size, however, there are the same types of facilities mentioned earlier—shelving for books, housing for special kinds of equipment or materials so that they may be transported, record-keeping equipment, a place to check the materials out for use. There may not be tables and chairs, for the function of the bookmobile is not to stay so long in one spot that it takes root. Rather it is what the name suggests—to move the books along.

Information about the kinds of bookmobiles available and suitable for the various parts of the world is probably obtainable from the UNESCO offices closest to you or from the UNESCO headquarters in Paris. Many nations have extensive programs already operating to take books to people, and each kind of program is oriented to the people who are served. The programs, then, will vary. But each will function for its own purposes and its own public.

14

Operating The Libary

Circulation

One of the main purposes of establishing any library is to make the book materials available to the library patrons. Boys and girls, as the patrons of the library, should have access to the materials and should be permitted to borrow the library materials of school libraries. In fact, children should be encouraged to do so and a part of the library's program should be to help them select wisely.

It may be a bit disconcerting to think of the materials which have been so laboriously processed and prepared for the library as leaving the library. But such leaving is usually only temporary and the materials are returned. This process of circulating the materials from the library to the children should be an orderly one. It should be planned and understood both by those who will be working with the children in the library and those who will be taking care of the records of the disposition of the materials.

Some of the work done earlier now begins to take on meaning. The book cards are taken from their cases (the book pockets) and are put to use as records of which borrower is taking what materials. As the children select the books which they wish to use, the book is brought to the librarian. She checks to see that the card in the book is the correct one for the book; she asks the student to sign his name on the book card in the proper space. Then the book card and the date due slip, in the book, are stamped with the calendar date on which the book should be returned to the library. The child takes the book, to read, to enjoy, to possess for a time as "his". The librarian places the book card in the charging tray, behind the cardboard divider marked with the same date which has been stamped on the card (the due date), and here the card remains as a record of its whereabouts until the book is returned to the library.

At the time the book is returned, the process is reversed. The librarian accepts the book. The book is opened to the date due slip and the date—the last date on it—is checked. That is, it is noted. Then the librarian turns to the charging tray where the book cards for books in circulation are being housed. She finds the divider marked with the proper due date and looks behind it for the card which belongs with the returned book. When this card is found, it is placed back in the book pocket.

The book must then be returned to its proper place on the shelves. To do this, note the call number of the book, either on the inside or the outside of the book. Go to the section of the library where books within this classified group are shelved and, checking the books on the shelf and comparing them with the returned book, find the correct place. Within the correct numbered group, you will recall, books are shelved by author's name. Repeat: First by classification number and then, within the same classified group, by author. When the proper place is found, return the book to the shelf. The process may, then, be repeated.

Record Keeping

Practically all librarians prepare, at regular intervals, a report for the individual or group to whom they are accountable. School librarians may prepare reports for principals of schools; librarians for institutional libraries probably prepare their reports for administrative heads of the institutions; the kind and frequency of the reports depend upon what these people wish to know and differ from each other.

Such reports are necessary to describe the work of the library and to point out its accomplishments as well as it needs. It may also provide the basis for evaluating the program and for providing whatever is essential for improvement. In order to be able to fulfill this kind of responsibility, it is important for the library to have certain facts at hand. These facts are best kept, day by day, recorded and summarized, and then made available at the time when the report is being prepared. Some kinds of factual information which are significant for every library include the items described below.

a. Circulation Record. At the end of each day a count should be made of the number of each of the different kinds of materials which have been borrowed from the library. Sometimes this accounting, in a large library, is kept by classification groups, and sometimes it is as simple as just one number to indicate how many items left the library. This record may be kept in a record book, especially prepared for this purpose; it may be kept in a notebook in which items of information are recorded; it may be a file of slips, each containing the information pertaining to that day.

Generally, it is a good idea to keep a running record, day by day, of the number of books of fiction, the number of books non-fiction, the number of other kinds of materials (such as magazines) borrowed on that day. This can be done by counting the book cards (for books) and the circulation file cards (for all other materials). Here is one kind of form which can be prepared easily.

DAILY STATISTICS...

Date:...............................

Attendance:................................

CIRCULATIONS: Fiction:.....................

Non-Fiction:.....................

Magazines:.....................

Audiovisuals:.....................

Other:.....................

DAILY TOTAL:.....................

BUDGET: Cleared for payment: Books.....................

Supplies.....................

Furniture.....................

Equipment.....................

SPECIAL WORK ACCOMPLISHED:

b. Attendance Record: You will note that the sample form contains only one line for attendance records. If it is considered important to keep track of attendance by the various periods of the day or the hours of the day, this kind of break-down can be included in the attendance record. This information, along with the circulation record, constitutes the most important information required to indicate the extent of work which the library performs.

c. Work Performed: It is sometimes requested that reports also include some statement concerning the number of books processed, the number of reference questions answered, the number of magazines prepared for circulation, or other information concerning special services. Some of these services which are normally a part of the library program include: 1. developing reading lists for special uses. 2. planning special exhibits with the library patrons for special interests. 3. developing and arranging exhibits. 4. ordering materials of various kinds, including books, and preparing the requisitions. 5. processng materials. 6. organizing or correcting or weedng files. 7. taking inventories. 8. evaluating and selecting books after inventories (to bring collections into balance). 9. answering reference problems. 10. providing reading guidance. 11. teaching library reference or research skills. 12. providing research materials.

d. Budget Records: When other peoples' moneys are being used for any purpose, it is extremely important that anyone involved in their expenditures keep an accurate record of how much is spent and for what. Whenever materials are received, there must also be a reconciliation of the charges with the amount actually paid. This record keeping is explained for book receipts on page 38. The same method may be used for reporting on other types of expenditures and receipts. These would include record keeping for expenditures for magazines, supplies, equipment, furniture, office supplies, materials for repairing books, etc.

e. Problems and Their Disposition: Very often it is only the accomplishments of a department which are reported. In the operation of libraries, it is equally important to know what problems have arisen, how they have been solved, what steps have been taken to try to solve them, how changes may prevent the development of problems. Improvements come, usually, as the result of planning to try to solve problems. It is urgent to recognize problems, for until there is knowledge of what the problem really is, there can be only the accidental solution.

Generally, in accumulating material and information for reporting purposes, it is advisable to consult with the administrator to whom the report will be made and to whom the library operation is responsible. If there is an indication of what will be needed before the time comes to make the presentation, this will, in itself, be one problem which will not arise.

Communication

Not only is the library a center of materials which communicate ideas, but it is also a center which needs to be communicated about. Its users and its administrators need to be informed about what it has and what it is doing. The record-keeping which has been described provides one kind of information which needs to be passed along to theirs. It may be equally important to let others know of new additions to the collections, what materials have been discarded, what services the library can offer, the hours of service, special needs of the library, and anything else which will build an understanding of the program.

There are several different ways of informing people, too. Newspaper articles or announcements; posters; verbal announcements to club groups; invitational exhibits; word of mouth communication; local radio stations; bulletins of other organizations—wherever people are concerned there is a ready-made channel of information, as well as a potential user.

Evaluating the Services

There are both formal and informal ways to evaluate a library's services. It is also possible to develop long and elaborate forms to use in going through this process. For a small library, for one whose purposes are fairly well outlined, there are several pertinent questions which can be applied to the situation and give an accurate picture of it.

1. Is the library doing what it is supposed to do?

2. Does the library have enough books and other materials to do its job?

3. Is the library collection housed so that the users can get to the materials they need for their purposes?

4. Is the atmosphere of the library one which makes people want to use it?

5. Is the library busier than it should be and are the demands for service so great that it is impossible to meet all these requests?

If the answer to these questions is "yes", undoubtedly the library is doing a job which people want done. And if some of the questions are answered "no" it will be well to take a look at the problems and see if somehow new solutions can be found.

Probably the best evaluation of the library and its program of service is what others thing of it. When the users of the services applaud, it's good.

UNESCO LIBRARY DEVELOPMENT

PROJECT

Mrs. Marguerite Summers, Acting Head of the Library Development Project of UNESCO, has available on request an extensive file of resource people and organizations in the various countries of the world. The countries, the library administrators, and the institutions listed below represent a very small part of this list. Mrs. Summers address is: UNESCO, Place de Fontenoy, Paris, France.

Australia	Australian Library Association c/o Public Library of New South Wales Margrave Street Sydney, Australia
China	Library Association of China c/o National Central Library 43 Nan-Hai Road Taipei, Taiwan, China
Denmark	Mr. Allerslov-Jensen Inspectorate of Public Libraries Odensegade 14 Copenhagen, Denmark
Great Britain	British National Book Center School Libraries Association (and British Library Association) Mallet House, W. C. 1 London, England International Federation of Library Associations Mr. Anthony Thompson 13 Vine Court Road Sevenoaks, Kent, England
Germany	Mr. William Scherf, Director Internatioanle Jungendbiblbotek Kaulbachstrasse lla Munchen ZZ
India	D.K. Kalia, Director of Libraries Delhi Public Library Queen Road Delhi, India

Japan	Takashi Ariyama, Secretary General (1961)
	Japan Library Association
	     Secretariat: UNEO Library
	                    UNEO Park
	Toito-Ku
	Tokyo, Japan

Kenya	East Africa Library Association P.O. Box 2022 Nairobi, Kenya
Netherlands	Mele, A. J. Muerkerchen vis der Muelen, Director Bureau Bock en Seugdder CV Badhuiskade 27 Scheveningen, Netherlands

New Zealand	Mr. G.T. Allen, director National Library Service Wellington, New Zealand
Norway	Mr. Anders Anderassen, Director of Libraries Department of Education Parkveren 41 b Oslo, Norway
Paris	UNESCO Place De Fontenoy Paris, France
Senegal	Library Association of Africa Association Internationale pour le Developpement des Bibliotheques en Afrique Borte Postale 166 Saint Louis, Senegal, Africa
Sweden	Mr. Bengt Halstrom, Director Malmo Stadsbibliotek Malmo, Sweden Miss B. Byland, Director Childrens Department

Index

India. UNESCO Lib. Dev. Project,
179
Instituto di Patologia del Libro
(Rome, Italy), 152
Inventory processes, 141-5
Invoices for orders, 49-51

J

Japan. UNESCO Lib. Dev. Project,
179
Jobbers, services in buying, 31, 35
Jobbers orders, procedures
Purchase orders, 48
Requisitions, 29, 30, 32
Joint authors, 95, 117

K

Kalia, D. K. India. UNESCO Lib.
Dev. Project, 179
Kenya. UNESCO Lib. Dev. Pro-
ject, 179

L

Library facilities, 159 ff
Characteristics, 161, 165
Location, 163-4
Materials' requirements, 161-2
Relation to use, 160 ff
Safety, 165
Storage space, 163
work space, 163
Library of Congress, U.S.
Library of Congress number, 46
Printed catalog cards, 44, 46, 51,
77
Legal aspects of school libraries, 23,
31
Library supply dealers, 37
Lost books, 141, 143, 144

M

Maintenance of collections, 150 ff
Mending books, 151-2
Muerkerchen vis der Muelen, Mele
A. J. Netherlands. UNESCO Lib.
Dev. Project, 179

N

National Archives, Washington,
D.C. 152
Netherlands. UNESCO Lib. Dev.
Project, 179
New Zealand. UNESCO Lib. Dev.
Project, 180
Norway. UNESCO Lib. Dev. Pro-
ject, 180

O

Order cards
Arrangement for requisitioning, 26
Checking for printed catalog
cards, 51
Information necessary, 25
Preparing, 41
Use as work card, 51, 88
Order directs, 32-35
Purchase orders, 48
Requisitions, 28
Order slips, 30
Ordering procedures, 31 ff
Out-of-print titles, 23
Out-of-stock titles, 23
Ownership marks
Stamp forms, 35-6
Use in processing, 60-2

P

Packing slips, see Invoices
Parent Teacher Association, 2
Paste, 35
Payment procedures, 38
People, as subjects of books, 130
Plastic covers
Applying call numbers, 89
Book pocket placement, 59
How to apply, 66-68
Marking spine of book, 63, 65
Preservation of materials, 152 ff
Prices, net and list, 32
Processing sequences, 53 ff
Processing services of agencies and
companies, 35
Pseudonyms, 92-3
Publishers
Catalogs, 35
Lists and addresses, 19, 34
Purchase orders, 48

R

Receiving book shipments
Checking invoices, 50
Clearing for payment, 51
Clearing requisitions, 50
Sequence of processes, 47 ff
Reference books, processing, 56
Requisitions
Arranging order cards for typing,
26
Information necessary, 27
Relation to purchase orders, 48,
49-52
Types of requisition forms, 27-30
Uses of requisitions, 27-30
Rules for filing catalog cards, 128-
30